Sinister Wisdom
Spring 2019

Publisher: Sinister Wisdom, Inc.
Editor: Julie R. Enszer
Graphic Designer: Nieves Guerra
Board of Directors: Roberta Arnold, Tara Shea Burke, Cheryl Clarke, Julie R. Enszer, J.P. Howard, Joan Nestle, Rose Norman, and Red Washburn

Cover Art: ByProduct IIA, Jane Bartier
Media: Rubber, pine, yarn, cotton, wool.
Size: Approx 30 x 30 cms

Artist Statement: Jane Bartier is a visual artist working particularly in response to place – Jane asks, what are our understandings of place, and how does place activate enquiry? From her practice of walking and looming she makes, from materials at hand, another landscape, markers of new maps. Jane lives on some fifty-seven acres west of Melbourne Victoria since mid-2017. This land is unceded Gulidjan country. In living on this land, recognising what has been, recognises stolen and lost knowledge. In her art practice, Jane responds to the terrain, boundaries, the space and air of this contested place where site experiences and the slow movement of walking yields up new ways of thinking, maybe new ways of being responsible as we live our future.
Jane's looming is developed

Notes for a Magazine 4
Letters to *Sinister Wisdom* 6
MARILYN HACKER
   Ghazal: The Dark Times 13
   Calligraphies VI 14
   After Forty Days ('Arbaoun) . 20
   Calligraphies X 22
JENNA LYLES
   Today's Suet, Tomorrow's Tallow . 27
   Egress 28
RITA MOOKERJEE
   A Man Threatens to Shoot Me on Behalf of 'Infidels for Trump' 29
   Venus As A Demon 31
ROSITA ANGULO LIBRE DE MARULANDA
   In Memoriam for Rita Angula Miret 32
CHRISTINA M. WELLS
   Last Stop Nursing Home Tour .. 38
MIE ASTRUP JENSEN
   The Moon 44
ALAINA SYMANOVICH
   Are You Even Gay? 46
JULIE WEISS
   On Our Wedding 50
MARISA CRANE
   Dancing With You 52
CHANICE CRUZ
   Last Kiss 53
   How to be Eaten by a Butterfly .. 54
EMEL KARAKOZAK
   Budding 1 56
   Budding 2 57

2 ♀ Sinister Wisdom 112- *Moon and Cormorant*

across a space of repetition, pattern, disruption and intervention. The works Jane produces can be long lengths of walked movement and small tube-like forms that are markers, or holders on a map.

Back Cover Art: Site Connections, Jane Bartier
Media: Rubber, twine, plastic, rope, cotton, wool.
Size: 3m x 45cm x 15cms

Subscribe online: www.SinisterWisdom.org
Join *Sinister Wisdom* on Facebook: www.Facebook.com/SinisterWisdom

Sinister Wisdom is a US non-profit organization; donations to support the work and distribution of *Sinister Wisdom* are welcome and appreciated. Consider including *Sinister Wisdom* in your will.

Sinister Wisdom, **2333 McIntosh Road, Dover, FL 33527-5980 USA**

Budding 5	58
Budding 7	59
Budding 9	60
Budding 10	61
Budding 11	62
Budding 12	63
Budding 13	64
Budding 14	66
Budding 16	68
Artist Statement	70

LILA TZIONA
I Think I'm in love with You but Please Don't Tell 71

KAYE LIN KUPHAL
Of Prayers 74

YEVA JOHNSON
Lavender Black 83
A Caste Released Offers Some Time in Contemplation 85
Coda to a Romantic Interlude .. 86
Poetic Sisters 87
Sinister Wisdom Says Hello ... 89

WINIFRED D. CHERRY
Catherine Nicholson and *Sinister Wisdom* 90

MINNIE BRUCE PRATT
Sweat, Sweet 99
Licked 100
The Tornado 101

TRIBUTE TO MICHELLE CLIFF
JULIE R. ENSZER
"Creating Alchemy": On the Work of Michelle Cliff 103

YASMIN TAMBIAH
Finding Michelle Cliff 117

Spring 2019 ♀ 3

SINISTER WISDOM,
founded 1976
Former editors and publishers:
Harriet Ellenberger (aka
Desmoines) and Catherine
Nicholson (1976–1981)
Michelle Cliff and Adrienne
Rich (1981–1983) Michaele
Uccella (1983–1984) Melanie
Kaye/Kantrowitz (1983–1987)
Elana Dykewomon (1987–1994)
Caryatis Cardea (1991–1994)
Akiba Onada-Sikwoia
(1995–1997)
Margo Mercedes Rivera-Weiss
(1997–2000)
Fran Day (2004-2010)
Julie R. Enszer & Merry
Gangemi (2010–2013)
Julie R. Enszer (2013–present)

ASHLEY-LUISA SANTANGELO
(Micro)Aggressions 119
RED WASHBURN
Cliff Notes: On Identity,
Memory, and Community .. 127
MICHELLE CLIFF
Claiming an Identity They
Taught Me to Despise 134

Snapshot Celebration
of Lesbian Love: Renate Klein
& Susan Hawthorne 142

Book Reviews 145

Contributors 168

Copyright © 2019
Sinister Wisdom, Inc.

All rights revert to individual
authors and artists upon
publication.

Printed in the U. S. on recycled
paper.

NOTES FOR A MAGAZINE

This year, 2019, is the beginning of my ninth editing and publishing *Sinister Wisdom*. I took on the project of editing *Sinister Wisdom* as a labor of love, beginning with the fall 2010 issue, *Sinister Wisdom* 81: *Lesbian Poetry—When? And Now!* At that time, I did not understand fully what being an editor for a periodical entailed. What I understood is that I loved *Sinister Wisdom*, and I wanted the journal to continue to publish and thrive. A few years later, when Susan Levinkind, now of blessed memory, could no longer do the administrative work of the journal, I took that work over becoming both editor and publisher of *Sinister Wisdom*.

Nine years into this odyssey, I still am not sure I fully understand the breadth and depth of the work of being an editor and publisher of a quarterly periodical. Nevertheless, with this issue, I have published thirty-two issues of *Sinister Wisdom*, inching up to a total of a third of all issues published. When I look back on the published issues, which I can see easily from desk on a special shelf in my office, I am proud, extraordinarily proud, of what I have accomplished with the journal and with an array of guest editors, volunteers, and dedicated dykes. I enjoy publishing publishing *Sinister Wisdom* immensely; it is one of the great pleasures in my life, and I am proud of the work of *Sinister Wisdom*. My intention is to continue as the editor and publisher of the journal until at least the fiftieth anniversary of *Sinister Wisdom* in 2026. At that point, I will be thinking about transitions and who will be taking up the mantle after me so that *Sinister Wisdom* can continue to publish wise and sinister work to ignite lesbian imaginations for generations to come.

In the past six months, more people have been writing to me about the journal, its contents, the quality of its contents, the substance of its contents. Lesbians agree with particular pieces and writers, and they disagree with other pieces and writers. And

Spring 2019 ♀ 5

they all talk about it. Passionately. This observation will surprise no one who has been around lesbian communities for a while: lesbians have a lot of opinions and they are happy to share them! It is a delight to hear from readers of and subscribers to the journal. In addition to the private conversations that people have with me on email and through the mail, there are lively conversations at our *Sinister Wisdom* Facebook page (I will confess that the conversations on Facebook both energize and annoy me!). The conversations that are unfolding, some represented in the pages of this issue, feel like a new development in my stewardship of the journal. Perhaps more women are tuning into our work? Perhaps the next incarnation of passionate and intense lesbian literary and political activism is brewing? I hope so! And I hope *Sinister Wisdom* will be an important part of the mix.

This issue of the journal, *Sinister Wisdom* 112: *Moon & Cormorant*, brings together fantastic writing from lesbians around the globe. In these pages are some poems by two of my favorite poets, Marilyn Hacker and Minnie Bruce Pratt, long-time friends of *Sinister Wisdom*, as well as work by new writers who excite and energize me.

I am also pleased to present a special tribute to Michelle Cliff at the end of this issue. Cliff edited *Sinister Wisdom* and brought her literary expertise and business acumen to the project for a few years in the early 1980s. She died in 2016. I am honored to reprint one of her influential essays alongside a few tributes to her and her work.

Enjoy this issue of *Sinister Wisdom*—and as always, tell me what you think! Thank you for your support for this journal and for the overall endeavor of promoting lesbian literature, art, and creativity in our world.

In sisterhood,
Julie R. Enszer, PhD
April 2019

LETTERS TO *SINISTER WISDOM*

10/17/18
Hi, Julie,

I have been reading the Trump issue with great interest and sadness, as I happened to open up to the page in which I saw Shanta Myers and Brandi Mells' faces appear on a poster of murdered black women. I gasped. I had forgotten that our personal pain had become a national news story. As you may or may not know, I live in the City of Troy. Last November, Shanta played the role of the turkey in our well-attended Thanksgiving Day foot race called the Turkey Trot. You couldn't miss Brandi, as she often strolled around town with the kids. And, JJ (Jeremiah), as he was known, was once in one of my poetry workshops at the Troy Boys and Girls club. Everyone in Troy knew JJ, and we often said he'd be our first black mayor! He always stood out and was a shining star. The four people that were brutally murdered were well known and loved by us in our pretty city. Their violent murder shocked, appalled and devastated the community that resides in this small city that lies along the Hudson River, and the GoFundMe page that staff from the Troy Boys and Girls Club set up quickly surpassed and exceeded its goal. What "quadrupedaled" the pain of this event was the revisionist and religious approach the Myers family took after Shanta's death. Quickly, once the funds reached a significant portion, Shanta's lesbianism was made invisible, and they would not share any of the funds raised for the four funerals with the Mells family, who were significantly worse off than the Myers family was in terms of funds. For those of us in the LGBT community here, that behavior gutted us in a way that only deepened the pain of these senseless murders. At the same time, many who did not know "us" thought the Troy Police Department would not handle this quadruple murder case well, clearly not knowing that Captain John Tedesco held a marriage celebration for my spouse and me when he learned that our own family had not. John is a long-time LGBT advocate. Later on, he personally told me that the crime scene was the most violent and vicious he had ever seen in his 43 years of police service, and all of this tragedy was over an Xbox. In the end, it was only when the executive director of a local LGBT organization for people of color (In Our Own Voices) stepped up and opened and managed a GoFundMe account for the family of Brandi Mells that we were able to help her family bury Brandi with dignity. Seeing their photographs in *Sinister Wisdom* brought this deep pain back to me, but I was relieved, too, because someone besides us in the City of Troy were saying their names. You can still see Teddy bears and balloons in front of their former residence at 158 Second Avenue, and I think about JJ and Shanise all of the time. I drive by their place of murder at least once a day to go from my home to a friend's house. I will never get them out of mind. Please ask the women who wrote the article to say their names out loud as many times as possible. I cannot begin to tell you how much these murders have affected us and continue to do so to this day. I saw the signs for the Turkey Trot on the way to work this morning, and I just started to cry. The only comfort we have is to remember them: *Brandi, Shanta, JJ and Shanise, I say your names every day.*

In Community,
Nancy Klepsch
Troy, NY

Dear Julie,

I have finally had time to read the Fall Journal, Dump Trump—Legacies of Resistance. I found it to be movingly informative, as well as all inclusive of our times. Very educational and extremely well done. It may be the best issue to date.

I was especially moved by Joan Nestle, but who wouldn't be? Her piece " Lesbian Polemics, Without Apology" was quite exceptional, even for her.

You should be very proud of the work that the Journal is doing under your care. I know that the work is a form of love, from you to your community. I just wanted to thank you once again for sharing your love and energy with the rest of us. It does not go unnoticed.

We are all living through an incredible time. We may not, as yet, have won the war on Fascism, but I do believe we are winning the battle against ourselves.

Be well - Be Happy

In Sisterhood,
Jill Crawford

Dear Editors,

I am disappointed and dismayed by some of the content in this issue. Most especially by the forty, yes 40!, pages of "Queer Suicidality, Conflict, and Repair". But also other pieces which have transgender as a focus. I was shocked to see this material in *Sinister Wisdom*, which I have supported, been published in, and cherished, as LESBIAN SPACE for many many years.

I decided to have a look at some past issues of the magazine which I have yet in my collection. I do not have all the issues from all the years, but I am fascinated by what I found. Usually on the inside of the front cover, sometimes on the next page, appeared what I would call a mission statement, or intention of the magazine. This was a fairly consistent statement over the years.

Spring 2019 ♀ 9

In issue #56 , Summer/Fall 1995, the first line of the statement reads:

Sinister Wisdom is a multicultural, multi-class, born-woman lesbian space.

Jumping up to #80, Summer 2010, the first line reads:

Sinister Wisdom is a multi-cultural, multi-class, female-born lesbian space.

But in issue #104, Spring 2017:

Sinister Wisdom is a multi-cultural, multi-class, lesbian space.

I do not know how that line appeared between Summer 2010 and Spring 2017, but somewhere in there the identity of lesbian being woman/female born was deleted. And the next issue I have is the current one, #110, Fall, 2018. Not only is the lesbian identity paled, there in fact is no mission/intention statement at all!! And it is in this issue that forty pages are devoted to a totally transgender topic.

Now I must hurry and say that I understand the importance of this article in and of itself, that suicide among transgender people is something to be acknowledged and understood, focused on, cared about, ministered to. BUT NOT IN LESBIAN SPACE!!

The front cover of this issue #110 has a line beneath the title of the magazine: A Multicultural Lesbian Literary & Arts Journal. And I noticed the envelope provided for donations does indeed specify lesbian space. The paragraph on that donation envelope reads:

Sinister Wisdom is a multi-cultural, multi-class, lesbian space. We seek to open, consider and advance the exploration of community issues. We recognize the power of language to reflect our diverse experiences and to advance our ability to develop critical judgement, as lesbians evaluating our community and our world.

So as I look at all this, I cannot help but think that here is yet another place where Lesbian space is being erased. Oh, the words, lesbian space still appear, but given the content of this issue and this statement on the donation envelope, I detect that our so-called space is being eroded, diversified; that we are to be taught how to "develop critical judgement"; that "our diverse experiences" now should include transgender experiences.

I mourn the loss of what has been so long a dependable place for female-born Lesbians to be published, a sure place where one can read strictly Lesbian content.

Or shall I hope that *Sinister Wisdom* gets back on track and performs her long standing service?

Very Sincerely,
Madrone

Thursday, 10 January 2019
(Hawk) Madrone
PO Box 593
Myrtle Creek, OR 97457

Dear Madrone,

Thank you so much for your correspondence from November 6, 2018. My apologies for the tardiness of this reply. I have had a very busy couple of months and I wanted to give your letter the time and attention it deserves.

First, thank you for your continued support for *Sinister Wisdom* and for your close attention to the journal and our publishing work. It is an honor to have readers and people in the community who care passionately about the journal.

You exactly are correct in the change of the statement of purpose about the journal. When I became the editor and publisher, I eliminated the words "female-born." These words are a descriptor that are divisive in our lesbian communities and, at the time that I dropped the word phrase, it was a flashpoint phrase that trans activists used to target lesbian-based publications and community organizations. My intention when I started editing the journal in 2010 and today is to keep *Sinister Wisdom* publishing, thriving, and serving the diverse ideas, interests, and needs of lesbians.

More than that desire to avoid divisive conversations about trans issues and trans inclusion in the journal at that time, I also dropped the idea of, as you phrase it, that "the identity of lesbian being woman/female born" because that is not congruent with my politics or my experience in the world. I came out in 1987 under conditions of coalition building between lesbians and gay men, among lesbians and gay men and bisexual people, and among lesbians, gay men, bisexual, and transgender people. I believe in those politics, even as I believe in enterprises dedicated to lesbians, enterprises like *Sinister Wisdom*, and various forms of separatist politics. Given my belief in politics of coalition and respect and responsiveness to people with shared interests and agenda and my recognition that the term "female-born" or "woman-born" is a term founded to divide and exclude, I eliminated it from the statement of the journal.

This decision is congruent with decisions of editors over the past forty years to shape *Sinister Wisdom* in ways that speak to their hearts and minds and to provide a journal that speaks to a broad and constantly changing lesbian community. *Sinister Wisdom* has published a variety of voices over the past forty-three years, including work by lesbians, work by heterosexual women who express "lesbian imagination," work by gender non-conforming people, work by gender queer women, work by incarcerated women, and much, much more. My commitment is to continuing the journal and continuing to nurture lesbian communities through publishing work.

For some women, lesbian space includes transgender women. A variety of lesbian spaces, organizations, and communities are grappling with these issues and reaching their own conclusions

12 ♀ Sinister Wisdom 112- *Moon and Cormorant*

and boundaries around the issues, just like *Sinister Wisdom* is and will continue to do.

Sinister Wisdom is edited by a diverse, eclectic group of women. For some women, the inclusion of trans voices and trans experiences is vital to the evolving conversations. Other women chafe at these inclusions. These conflicts seem to me part of the reality of being in community, of reading and thinking together, and of being open about different opinions, ideas, and visions for the world. Your opinion is appreciated and valued. As are other opinions.

Nothing in *Sinister Wisdom* 110: *Dump Trump*, or the past eight years of publishing that I have done at *Sinister Wisdom* with now over thirty issues published erases lesbians or lesbian space. Rather, the journal expands the space for lesbians by meeting a regular publishing schedule, increasing from three issues a year to four issues a year, expanding the size of the journal, increasing the number of subscribers, and adding the **Sapphic Classics** series, which brings attention anew to classic lesbian books, among many other activities that nurture and promote lesbian art, literature, and culture.

I am proud of the work that *Sinister Wisdom* has done to build a multi-cultural, multi-class lesbian space and this work will continue, I hope for the next forty-three years. I believe we are on track and performing the long-standing service womandated by the journal.

I will be printing your letter and my response in the next issue of Sinister Wisdom, Sinister Wisdom 112. Thanks always for your support. I hope this letter finds you well and thriving!

In sisterhood,
Julie R. Enszer, PhD

GHAZAL: THE DARK TIMES

Marilyn Hacker

Tell us that line again, the thing about the dark times...
"When the dark times come, we will sing about the dark times."

They'll always be wrong about peace when they're wrong about justice...
Were you wrong, were you right, insisting about the dark times?

The traditional fears, the habitual tropes of exclusion
Like ominous menhirs, close into their ring about the dark times.

Naysayers in sequins or tweeds, libertine or ascetic
Find a sensual frisson in what they'd call bling about the dark times.

Some of the young can project themselves into a Marshall Plan future
Where they laugh and link arms, reminiscing about the dark times.

From every spot-lit glitz tower with armed guards around it
A huckster pronounces his fiats, self-sacralized king, about the dark times.

In a tent, in a queue, near barbed wire, in a shipping container,
Please remember *ya akhy*, we too know something about the dark times.

Sindbad's roc, or Ganymede's eagle , some bird of rapacious ill omen
From bleak skies descends, and wraps an enveloping wing about the
dark times.

You come home from your meeting, your clinic, make coffee and look
in the mirror
And ask yourself once more what *you* did to bring about the dark times.

ACKNOWLEDGEMENT:

"Ghazal: The Dark Times" by Marilyn Hacker, originally appeared on the Academy of American Poets' Poem a Day site. Used with permission of the author.

CALLIGRAPHIES VI

Marilyn Hacker

After disaster
(again) in her small skylit
sublet, N. simmers

lentils while she reads a long
book about Ibn Arabi.

In prison they made
chess pieces out of stale bread.
She taught the women

to play. Their first champion was
an apolitical thief.

**
Political grief,
apolitical despair,
or it's vice versa –

either way, insomnia.
Rapping on the neighbors' door,

three in the morning—
no, it's seven, and still dark.
One of the roommates

next door home from a night I'm
too tired out to imagine.

**

Imagine language
after opaque years
become transparent...

since the hour needs witnesses
who can construct a sentence.

Which was my country?
A schism in the nation,
slogans on banners

while a compromised future
slouches towards investiture.

**
Towards light again, when
wet snow is falling on the
January sales.

The chestnut stairs gleam, but
I'm short of breath, knees give way.

My ideal reader
doesn't read English, and I've
stalled in her language

— or his—while he/she stares at
an impassable border.

**
Bored or despairing
or enduring a headache,
and humid winter.

A book I loved; a reproach:
You read like a three-year-old.

The masters dying,
their festive midnight children
blown out like fireworks.

A constriction in the chest.
An explosion in the street.

* *

One Hundredth Street sun-
lit on election morning:
another country

that seemed possible again.
I went to the Baptist Church

to vote – lines, laughter,
scowls, polyglot commotion,
then, fresh air. That night

I read Hannah Arendt till
bad news muddied late daybreak.

**

Bad news for heroes
chain-smoking across borders,
not out of danger.

She smoked outside the café—
it drizzled as we read her

piece for an-Nahar;
rolled cigarettes at demos
between her speeches.

She writes in the ward bed with
a chemo port in her chest.

**
Not a port city
but the river is always
lumbering through it

on its muddy way elsewhere,
banks erased often by rain.

We crossed a bridge in
a shurba of languages.
History trundled

beneath, gravel on a barge,
ground down to its origins .

**
Ground beef sautéed with
onions and tomatoes, then
add frozen okra

N. was so pleased that we found
at the Syrian grocer's

near Faidherbe. Why no
okra in Indian food
in France, we wondered ?

18 ♀ Sinister Wisdom 112- *Moon and Cormorant*

Bindhi, bamiyaa. A pot of
white rice swells on the burner.

**

Swells and then explodes,
"like a raisin in the sun,"
our impatience, and

others'. Five years ago, in
some café, after some demo,

the Algerian,
Zinab, told the Syrian,
Aïcha, you'll have

what we had, ten black years of
slaughter. And Aïcha wept.

**

Did not cry when I
fell on my face, scraped my chin
and turned my ankle,

or when the midnight and the
morning emails announced death –

a younger man, an
older woman, Berkeley and
Brooklyn, unanswered

letters from two coasts. I took
two pills for my aching face.

**

The two young women
come up the stairs with parcels,
their conversation

punctuated by laughter.
The old woman is coughing

in her apartment.
One of them opens the door.
They can't, she can't know

their white nights' precipices,
her dictionaries' questions.

ACKNOWLEDGEMENTS:

"Calligraphies VI" by Marilyn Hacker, originally appeared in *PN Review* (UK)
and on the Poetry Daily website. Used with permission of the author.

AFTER FORTY DAYS ('ARBAOUN)

Marilyn Hacker

She called you "My lovely," as you writhed, dying
in atrocious pain that the morphine top-ups
eased for half an hour, and I thought of Tadmor
where you had comrades,

but the Darwish lines I memorized with you
where a mother sings for her martyr's wedding
weren't where I wanted them, on my tongue, if
words could have reached you.

It's too easy to costume you as Zainab
led in chains to Damascene exile (you were
Damascene by adoption, missed the city
more than Lattakié).

Exile, first your refuge, became your torture
as the months passed, added up years, a window
fogged with possibilities gone nostalgic
despite your fierceness...

so you chain-smoked, as you harangued who'd listen
on the public squares, in a foreign language,
or spoke softly, friend at a café table
writing your own roles.

How his face, or hers, changed as you evoked it,
wiping dust and steam from a winter window,
the beloved, nameless beyond erasure,
multiple, murdered.

You became your distances, grew your hair long.
Eyes dark-circled, books stacked on shelves behind you,
you said, pale, three times, in dialect: I'm a
refugee, لاجئـة

CALLIGRAPHIES X

Marilyn Hacker

Like Jude the Obscure,
you wait beneath the vaulting
of a corridor

where you never belonged and
nothing here belongs to you.

How sallow your skin,
how outmoded your clothing,
how crumpled your face,

while multi-ethnic students
stroll past, bright-caparisoned.

**
How bright the past looks,
when that was being forty,
free, in an airport

on some Adonic journey
or in a more recent year

believing in the
revolution you kissed her,
kissed him away to—

Kafranbel's Friday demo
recounted to you in French.

**

The French woman who
can't go back to Damascus
shouted at her friend

the activist refugee:
The Kurds were right to keep out!

Now it's civil war!
The two Kurds – one's her husband—
said nothing. Around

us on the lawn, families
heard Arabic, and wondered.

**

I wonder about
my friend in Jerusalem.
Imru al-Qays is

his muse, if you will, and he
translates Palestinians.

A scholar my age,
protests what former exiles
inflict on exiles,

but why that street, that hill, in
all the diasporic world?

**

Diasporic grave,
narrow as a ploughed furrow,
elbowed in on both sides

by riverains of Montreuil
who lived and died there, while she

was housed there by chance:
political refugee's
right to a lodging —

accidental neighbourhood,
now her accidental tomb.

**
Tadmor tomb portraits,
the person's name and "Alas"
beside his, her face

in the little museum
in Hamra, empty today

brother and sister,
a distraught-looking lady,
a husband and wife,

Palmyra, empty today.
Khaled al-Asa'ad: Alas.§

**
Antigone was
a role for her, and I know
she played the part

in Arabic, as I saw
it played in Saint-Denis by

§ Khaled al-Asa'ad was the 83-year-old Syrian archaeologist who had worked all his life on the translations of the tablets of Ur at Palmyra/Tadmor, and was still working at this when he was beheaded by Da'esh at the site in August of 2015, and his body exhibited on the public square.

Palestinian
actors. In Damascus, she
was in a theatre.

Then they were outside, the stage
built in haste, the words her own.

**
There was a word I
didn't know in your letter,
almost a friend's name,

one character different. I
looked it up, and it means death.

The rebel who tied
her wild hair back to speak at
Fadwa's funeral

is gone, forty-nine, no one
quite knows how, why. Some love kills.§

**
Some lovely useless
ubiquitous foreign word,
bougainvillea

blooming well into July,
framing blue vistas of sea.

An orange cat walks
by. There are hundreds, not strays
but the descendants

of civil war survivors
abandoned in this barzakh.

§ "Some love kills" من الحبّ ما قتل is an Arabic proverb.

26 ♀ Sinister Wisdom 112- *Moon and Cormorant*

**

Stacked in abandon
of any order but what
might catch the eye, books

you now imagine reading,
al-Jahiz and al-Ma'ari

and here, this woman
an essay revealed to you,
dead too soon, poems

a dictionary lights up
as you probe among the roots.

**

If Abiah Root[§]
had kept writing letters to
her friend Emily

after she moved to Beirut,
and if Emily wrote back...

Amherst to Beirut —
birds of imagination
circle the Corniche,

invisible ink quatrains:
where, *with them, would harbour be?*

§ Abiah Root was a girlhood friend of Emily Dickinson when Emily was briefly sent to boarding school at what is now Mount Holyoke College. They corresponded after Emily returned to Amherst. In her twenties, Abiah married the Reverend Daniel Bliss, and went with him to Lebanon, then part of "Greater Syria," where he founded what was first called the Syrian Protestant College in 1866, and remained at its head till 1902. It is now the American University of Beirut. The very last words of the poem, in italics, are a quote from Dickinson.

TODAY'S SUET, TOMORROW'S TALLOW

Jenna Lyles

Through the fence
    her thighs were latticed

and her depressed cot sprang back
    to slated fugue.

    Outside:

low-care posies consumed
    a fecund plot seldom browsed.

The sun broke over her knees
    finite, blinding.

The silage stilled in her rumen
    as her divine bulk was lit from atop.

EGRESS

Jenna Lyles

I.
derived from the viscid sap
of resin breasts barking

by eventide tempered

II.
the unbranched oryx
wastes her winter estrus
a c q u i e s c i n g

III.
raxed to popping
the virgin stamen
bursts

 pollen & papillae

   cynosure of lilac tongues

A MAN THREATENS TO SHOOT ME ON BEHALF OF 'INFIDELS FOR TRUMP'

Rita Mookerjee

Infidels for Trump reminds me of the Aryan Brotherhood
but I guess the latter is worse. The paradox is obvious

but this is the problem with people who don't read books.
Now don't get on me about class issues and freedom of speech.

You know what freedom looks like? The library where unlike my house,
everyone is welcome. He should have taken advantage of that.

Here's a tip: when you turn to talk shit to a brown chick in a bar,
make sure you're not speaking her language. I mean literally,

speaking her language because while you talk about Aryan
Arya is a Sanskrit word that means exalted which is the last thing

that white people were if we look at technology, advancement,
and dental hygiene. The real irony is that it was my people

who came down from the Caucus mountains. The swastika
is the symbol of my goddess, the one who wears a belt

of severed male heads. My people invented numbers and bathing.
The characters in your holy scripture looked just like me

which I know isn't a problem for the Infidel for Trump and it's that
classic redneck confidence that is beautiful. A complete alliance

to the most flawed ideals, deep love for a flag that looks so much like
the Union Jack it borders on adorable. And so I fold my glasses and say

30 ♀ Sinister Wisdom 112- *Moon and Cormorant*

to the meathead decked out in red: I don't know if you know this,
but you lost. You lost and you continue to lose. You rep those colors

in Florida, a notorious traitor state, where men hid
in the salt plants, sunk into swamp mud, jumped to the gulf

and tried to swim to Mexico rather than suffer Robert E. Lee's bullshit
never mind the couple thousand that said fuck it and joined the
Union troops?

And don't get me started on Donny boy because those jokes write
themselves
and unlike you, I'm no fucking cliché so read a book then come through

and see me sometime, big boy. A black cat will laugh in the doorway
when you drop your PF-9 once I go to work on those Infidel knees

because you people always have the same two problems: no book
learning
and a total lack of imagination which is why you won't expect

my Louisville slugger: the icon of a favorite pastime
and I don't mean baseball because I'm not America

I'm not Southern I'm a brown girl and a violent bitch and a loud cunt
my only hobbies are breaking necks and smashing kneecaps

so when you come through be ready to give me that good head
and I don't mean get ready to eat this good pussy you'll never be so blessed

what I mean is watch your neck because I've got plenty
of room on my belt for you.

VENUS AS A DEMON

Rita Mookerjee

After I said I didn't mind
I hid in the nightviolets
watching the new lovers in clairvoyant
silence. My teeth threatened to
popcorn out of my gums.

> *I take pride*
> *in being*
> *easily incensed.*

I considered how Cleopatra
who was not Egyptian
had servants mash a cucumber
with honey and slather it
in a spiral across her back.
they'd leave with filmy
palms: a shared aphrodisiac.
Cleopatra didn't mind this
act of charity because
the water of the cucumber
would dry in a sugared
crust and her consorts would
find her naked and wreathed in bees.

> *that intuition*
> *that self-assuredness*
> *comes with being an outsider*
> *summoning bees and snakes:*
> *the best way to keep*
> *kissing cadavers*
> *out of my house.*

IN MEMORIAM FOR RITA ANGULA MIRET
Rosita Angulo Libre de Marulanda

Trigger Warning:
This is a true story about two young sisters finding love in each
other in a society that insisted that all sexuality ought to service the
patriarchy. They were met with a lot of violence.

It is hard to believe that once upon a time I held my lesbian body in chains. You never knew; you had your own issues going on. We were sisters in the same litter of 13 and another 3 sired elsewhere. Mother kept busy handing out hoards of orders and neglect in return. Father was often not present in mind though his body was faithfully in attendance. Sometimes he'd come up with some sweet things like asking us to comb his hair when we were fighting; he knew, somehow, that touching would make us feel better. So, we combed it and placed bobby pins on it so that we'd be touching him and facing each other in a semicircle as he leaned back on his chair. At other times he'd make agua de panela, that sweet Colombian drink made out of sugar loaf and lime juice. Grandmother was not interested in us; she had done her social duty of having one child—my mother—and was aghast that her child was now having so many. Grandma went as far as seeking assistance from the local priest who came to counsel mom and left her with a pamphlet on "the problem of too many children." Even the priest advocated that she stop having any more babies. As far as I know, the priest never counseled dad nor left any pamphlets with him. She was able to sparse the last three children putting a distance of four and five years between them—a drastic change after popping her first eleven babies nine months to two years apart. She finally succeeded getting the man off from top of her by placing her thirteenth child between them. That baby had no crib of his own but a huge function as prophylactic. It worked!

Puberty was so rough for us; we suffered our passage together as we were two years apart. I was the younger sibling. We were punished severely for being vulnerable females.—you being retarded and mute and I having been marked as lesbian since the age of four. And, here we were in the thicket of our physical changes and the threshold of womanhood. You were thirteen and I trailed behind you with eleven years of my own. We were all alone without assistance surrounded by hostile institutions that ruled our home; that forbade our sexuality; that ignored our intellectuality; that loathed our female presence. I saw mother take out her female self loathing on the guindo tree because it emanated an aroma much like her own. She had it chopped down for the same reason that certain species of gingko trees are so rare (except in buddhist monasteries) because of the funky female scent they emanate.

We shared a lot of the same mental luggage we were taking on this journey, you leading the way. I remember the day you invited me to have sex with you. How old were we? Six and eight? You must have known it was forbidden for you lured me under a plank that rested on one of the patio walls. I entered the square angled space where you laid beckoning me. When I joined you, you offered me the tip of a belt and your naked behind. Without words, I understood your request and was happy to oblige. You had such a gorgeous bottom. Your face was lit with delight. And, along came mother dashing from her entrepreneurial chores in the garage and started beating us up with her sandal. She beat me some but she beat you up ten times more severely. She beat you up so intensely because she knew how much I loved and cared for you. Through you, she could control me, too. She was making me responsible for both of our behaviors because, if I deviated, you would be punished more severely. I got the message loud and clear. I am sure you did, too, and we never engaged after that. I suspect our older sister snitched but I have no proof. I still relish the sweet moment I had with you before we got so rudely and violently interrupted. All power to you, my sister! All power to us! First playmates forever!

I remember fondly the sweet closeness we had for just a few minutes that has lasted me a lifetime though at times it is buried under tons of anger at having my sexuality and your sexuality trampled. We were not hurting anybody. Nor were you hurting anybody but having a great time, at thirteen, masturbating all over the place. Privacy was not something we were taught as we slept in our parents' room even as they were making babies. And, even if you hid now, as you hid us years earlier in the square angled space, you would be found. So, you threw caution to the wind—no use trying—and masturbated as we witnessed your horny activities. You took all the risk and never lured me, beckoned me, nor invited me to join you in celebration of womanhood and female pleasures. You spared me. And I knew better than to join you as it would make your act of rebellion ten times riskier.

But hell hath no more fury than a patriarch scorned at seeing a woman in pleasure without him. Not pleasuring him; not making babies for him. And you, in your young lesbian body, had nothing else to lose but your body. So, you owned it by touching it and pleasuring it. Please forgive me for outing you, you are safe now; may you rest in peace. I want the world to know the hateful extremes to which the evil patriarchs will go to thwart innocent childhood sexual explorations. You were made to live this drama of sex and violence at such a tender age and I was made to witness it, my sister, my first playmate, my love. Retarded, my foot! You fought for control of your body but they outnumbered you; they out powered you. I am so proud of you for fighting so fiercely!

I'm not sure if dad ever saw you masturbating but he'd hear you at night, snap, crackle and pop, and the whams when the shoe fell upon your eroticized flesh. This went on for about a year when you decided to strike back. Your beautiful body had grown and now you could strike back. I wish you had taken on father for not opposing mom but we suspected his passive agreement, perhaps his pleasure behind the scenes. I had a dream around that time that I still remember sixty-two years later. There was fecal matter spread over the patio's sink and dad was cleaning that up.

Multiple daily beatings would not make you stop. Mother was intent on "taking away your habit." Father had nothing to say though he was the one who read the papers and communed with others outside the house. Joseph Kennedy was the sales target of a lobotomist who destroyed Rosemary's brain just like dad was the sales target for the use of destructive psychiatric social control services. The selling point? Complete docility by the young women in question. Complete control of female sexuality by the patriarchy. I suspect dad made the connection with the professional heavy-weight muscle to tip the power unfairly against the innocent young woman that you were, retarded and mute, just entering into adulthood. I am sure the psychiatrists were paid plenty.

Mom told me, at the time, that the electroshock treatments you were getting were being administered at the municipal hospital which was run by the nuns; I was with them, in the car one time we picked you up at the hospital. They made sure I witnessed you after a treatment. You looked beaten; withdrawn. Your eyes had sunk. You smelled of ether. To me, this was all authorities breaking your young head! The municipal hospital was administered by the State, run by the Church, in which Doctors worked and, now, I had never heard of a Psychiatrist before. Electroshock sounded terribly severe to me, and it was. I was so frightened for you. I was so frightened for me because, what would they do to me if they knew that I was beginning to feel stirrings in my young female body? I, too, was coming of age.

In school, at the age of twelve, when seeing pies on the blackboard used to explain fractions, I would see your head being broken in pieces. I turned off to math for a few years even though math had been one of my favorite subjects. Because I took to crocheting, excessively, my peers began to call me "grandma." Previously a model student, I began to act out. I had so much anger.

Decades later I identified immediately with *Love and Rage,* one of the book titles by Gabriel García Márquez, our very own paisa. Strong emotions. Nobody to talk about them. Nobody to trust. Feeling betrayed by family, church, doctors, shrinks, and state at such a tender age, what does a young lesbian do but strike at her own body? I could not be punished because I would already be punishing myself. Still at twelve, holding all this love and rage inside me, I noticed the angry family dog that barked all day that was kept tied to a tree by a metal chain. Surely, I would need something that strong to hold such powerful feelings in check. So, I took one of its chains and put it tight around my waist and would sleep with it at night. It was very painful removing the chain in the morning and seeing all the indentation marks on my skin. This would be my secret I would contain deep within myself. The chain would become, not only the physical restraint from sexual activities and from acting out my rage, but also as the mental landmark I constructed to remember the set of events that led me to it.

Now, a word about mother's role; about her participation; about her cooperation. Cooperation is a female conditioning by nature and by nurture. It is by nature because nature has gifted women with the glue that holds the social seams together. Women are the creators of families and societies and we are the axle upon which every society runs. Cooperation is one of our working tools much like the spider weaves the web. We practice cooperation and teach it in order to make room for everyone; to make everyone comfortable, and to hold peace within our spheres. Cooperation is also nurtured because it is learnable and teachable and it gets passed on for generations. However, nurture also includes coercion, i.e., not nature. Given all the messages I received at the ring of fire with my sister, it was made clear to me, in no uncertain terms, what happens to angry and horny women. I surrendered my sexuality and my life to the patriarchy when I began to cause harm to my young lesbian body. I opted for cooperation whereas you fought back. I survived, you didn't. Surrender is forced cooperation. At the moment of self-harm, I surrendered control over my very own body and spirit; I was twelve going on thirteen. I am here to tell the tale for both of us. May you rest in peace.

It seems clear to me that mother was not in control of her body. Who knows what messages she was given at her own ring of fire. The priest gave her license to say, no, to our father, albeit passively until she took matters into her own hands and placed her last child between them. No means no! No more, you don't, you jerk! Using her young child as prophylactic, was an apologetic move but it would be the only kind of prophylactic her Church would not disapprove. She cooperated with Church mandate not to use contraceptives. I am sure that being used as prophylactic hurt that child, my youngest brother. Given the isolation of women in the patriarchal family structure, and given that women are nurtured (read coerced) into cooperating with the patriarchy and not with each other, she had no one to trust or discuss ways or means to deal with her distress. Thus, she surrendered her children: the youngest one as prophylactic and she surrendered the two girls in puberty to the torture the patriarchs meted out.

However, by taking back control of her own body, albeit slowly, my mother risked having her man visit prostitutes, thus losing some of his presence and some of the family wage. Prostitution is another forced cooperation. A prostitute cooperates with her pimp, with her john. She's essential to the patriarchy because she is held as a constant threat to wives for continued coerced cooperation with their husbands. If either woman doesn't cooperate, she has a whole set of consequences to suffer and, even if she cooperates, she has a whole lot of consequences to suffer. Neither woman can win.

© RositaAngulo Libre de Marulanda

LAST STOP NURSING HOME TOUR

Christina M. Wells

Nothing says "You're in a nursing home, and I'm not," quite like driving up in a BMW SUV. I regret that, and I tried to explain it to the rental counter. But when they decide they want to upgrade you, there's no stopping them, even when you can barely see over the wheel and have to go charging into a nursing home parking lot that's up a cliff from the river.

I was relieved to park. This was my fifth nursing home excursion that year, and I hadn't really wanted to end the tour in style. There's never a need to be cocky.

The front office was no help, which makes you feel great, when you're trying to locate a friend who is spending the rest of her life in a place. I signed in and walked to a centrally located nurses' counter. Central next to what, I thought. It was over the river and through the woods. So to speak.

"I'm looking for Laura Bettis," I said. I rattled my pink nails on the counter in front of me, making my ring shine in that nurse's face.

"Ms Bettis is in our memory unit." She looked over her computer with the authority of someone who had no idea what she was saying.

"She's what?" If I were being honest, I had heard her. I find that if I pretend to be a little deaf, I get a few minutes to pull my face together.

"The memory unit. It's around the corner. I'll need to let you in."

"She does see visitors?"

"Yes ma'am."

I don't know what I thought was wrong with her. I thought maybe she would have broken something. Something was broken, alright.

Spring 2019 ♀ 39

I entered her room. She had on a filmy pink robe over cat pajamas and was looking out the window, down at the water below. It was murky, like an idea of water without any actual liquid to push the waves along.

"Laura?"

An aide was folding up some old lady jeans and underwear. I wanted her to leave. Could I tell her to leave? Usually I didn't have to.

"GRANNY, YOU HAVE A VISITOR!" I had my hand on Laura's shoulder, so there was probably no need for the aide's stage scream.

"Do you know who I am?" I said.

"Hi, Virginia." She said it in the most natural way, as if she had seen me for lunch the day before.

"SHE USUALLY REMEMBERS PEOPLE SHE KNEW A LONG TIME AGO. DID YOU KNOW HER A LONG TIME AGO?"

"Yes. And I'm not deaf."

"BUT GRANNY IS!" This woman wore purple scrubs and clearly worked there.

"Vita, do you remember our trip to Venice?" Laura grinned.

"Nobody comes to see me," she said.

"NOW GRANNY, YOU KNOW THAT'S NOT TRUE! SOMEONE WAS HERE JUST YESTERDAY!"

"Vita, what do you remember about Venice?"

"I FIND IT'S BETTER IF PEOPLE CALL HER BY HER REAL NAME."

"I guess that's why you feel it necessary to call her Granny."

"We find it helps the patients if we refer to them by familiar family names."

"She didn't have any children. Hence no grandchildren."

"You almost fell out of the boat," Laura interrupted. This surprised me, like a parallel conversation beaming in from somewhere else.

40 ♀ Sinister Wisdom 112- *Moon and Cormorant*

"WHAT ELSE DO YOU REMEMBER, GRANNY?" Purple scrubs was curling up on the afghan at the foot of the bed, like this was story time.

"Do you have somewhere else you need to be?" I said.

"I find it helps the guests if I'm nearby."

"Believe it or not, this is not my first memory unit." This wasn't where I expected to be for Laura, though. I don't know where I thought she would be, but the others hadn't mentioned this.

"You almost fell out of the boat." Laura jumped in again.

"Yes, yes. That's right. I did. Do you remember why I almost fell out of the boat?"

"You stood up and said a poem in Italian."

I wondered how much of that she remembered. Did she know it was for her?

"Do you like your job?" Damn. Laura took us somewhere else. I had been looking for the refrain, something besides the boat I nearly fell out of while screaming an Italian sonnet. That day hadn't gone so well. But I didn't want to let the boat go, just the same.

"Well, I retired last year. But I liked it alright, I guess," I finally said.

"What did you do?

"I was a civil rights attorney." She knew that once.

"But you were happy?"

"I was happy when I helped people."

"Did you like your job?" I thought of answering differently, but I went for the condensed version of the last round.

"I was a civil rights attorney. I was happy when I got to help people."

"Did you like your job?"

"I worried constantly that I would never have enough money and that I would have to sell my soul to the devil to make enough. But I got to help people, and that made me happy."

"Did you like your job?"

"WHAT DO CIVIL RIGHTS ATTORNEYS DO?" Purple scrubs tilted her head to the side.

"Are you still here, dear?" I said. She scowled at me.

"GRANNY, I'M GOING TO RUN DOWN THE HALL. I'LL BE RIGHT BACK IF YOU NEED ANYTHING."

"Can you bring me a beer?"

"I THINK WE'VE ESTABLISHED I CAN'T BRING YOU BEER." She laughed like this was the funniest thing, an old lady wanting a beer. Laura always did like her beer.

Now Laura looked at me, clearing her throat. I didn't want to cover what I thought of my damn career. That's why people retire, so they can stop talking about it.

"Laura my Vita. . . I want to show you something." I held out my ring finger in front of her face.

"I finally got married. You know, it's possible now. Has been for a few years. Gloria and I decided to make honest women out of each other."

"Congratulations! Nice ring."

She stared out at the water. I couldn't look at that dirty water without thinking of Venice, and what it had meant to look out the window over it. This was a bad substitute, like city diarrhea over rocks.

Laura had married Mark, and Mark had died about fifteen years before in a man's bed. Laura had never had a whole lot to say about that, but then, what's to say? That sort of speaks for itself, I think. Or maybe it doesn't.

"You asked me to marry you once." It surprised me when that came out of her mouth, mostly because I had no memory of it whatsoever. I could swear that that never happened. Was I joking? Was she joking? Could she have me mixed up with someone else? What's worse is, could she have been thinking of Gloria?

"What do you remember about that? Are you sure?"

She laughed at me, twirling the end of a long gray hair. "You stood up on the boat, and we nearly all fell into the water. When you sat back down in the boat, you put your arm around me and said, "Let's run away together. . ."

Oh. That. That wasn't the same as a marriage proposal, but I did remember. I had taken off my sweater and wrapped it around her pale shoulders. Then I had talked about how Petrarch had recited poems for Laura. Laura was always in the distance, like she practically didn't exist. But she brought him to God.

About that moment, I heard church bells. I know, how convenient. But that town where she lived, and where she was dying, always had church bells. It was this crazy way of marking time, letting people know it was 10 am in case they had forgotten, or had no idea what time it was or where they were.

"I know that I loved you," she said. That was sudden. Forty years of trying, and it was past tense, in a nursing home, with a dirty river on the outside, a ring on my finger, and Purple Scrubs outside, screaming at some other woman who wasn't her grandmother.

"Are you sure about that?" I said. "I remember your pulling away from me when I said something to you in the boat."

She nodded, looking back out at the dirty water. We paused for a few minutes, and I thought we were sitting with an honest moment.

"I know that I loved you," she said again. Now I felt like we were rehearsing. I knew enough to know that we could go on like this all day, saying these kinds of phrases. I could have changed the conversation.

"I loved you, too." That time, I didn't think there was a whole lot left to say. My heart started beating, waiting for something else. I didn't know what else. I looked out at the water, and the rocks, and I couldn't get past the wide venetian blinds on the windows of a nursing home in Tennessee. This, I thought, is my reality check, not hers.

I placed my hand on Laura's shoulder. "My Vita, I have to go," I said. This was a weak way out, but I had no idea what I would say if we went for number three, and I hated the feeling that I was going over something and over it and over it, lining up something with the past.

Laura stood up from her chair, reaching her arms out to place them around me. I had to reach for her to hold her steady. She took my face, and I could tell from the look on hers that we were going for somewhere we had been before. But we didn't.

"Thank you for coming to see me. Always remember that I love you, Virginia."

I paused for a moment, thinking of her sitting back down in that chair, never remembering this moment, like I didn't remember what I must have said to her in the boat after we nearly knocked it over.

"I love you, too, Vita. Laura."

It took me a few minutes to remember that those locked wards usually have a button you can push to send you out into the rest of the world. I walked out into the lot, past the cars and to the gravel by the water below. I picked up rocks as I went, and I looked out past the water's edge to a boat that stood precarious in the middle, straight across from the window where an old woman with a thin pink bathrobe was sitting.

THE MOON

Mie Astrup Jensen

She was always so in love with the moon
The dark night sky surrounding it
A darkness that could take away
Any joy, any smile
Even our last breath
But that was the thing
The moon would shine
It would become brighter as darkness would
Take over and form silence
So enlightening, yet so mysterious
The moon would bring light
It would guide people on a journey
A journey to distant places
During a long walk
Sitting under the night sky
Or in a dream

The moon was attractive
Like an energy carried
By thousands of oxen
It was hypnotising her as she sat
Leaned against the tree
It intensified her magnificent curiosity
In darkness, she always found the light
A light to make her smile
To make her breathe
To make her shine
She mirrored herself in the moon
So powerful, yet so mysterious
It was in loneliness and darkness

She would find her light
Her mum had once told her that

It was in the midst of her solitude
That she would find herself
That she would see that she
Is powerful beyond measure
That even when darkness tries to
Hold her back
She has a friend in the moon
That she could be
So strong, yet so mysterious
Because she did not need the limelight
She would silently do the work
So that one day
People would look up and
Fall in love with her
The way she loved the moon

ARE YOU EVEN GAY?

Alaina Symanovich

my girlfriend asks as we face off in a closet
(–yes, a literal closet).

She accuses me of liking her best friend
because I got drunk and flirty with him

and I have so many rebuttals
molting in the back of my throat

that for a moment I am nothing but an aborted opinion.
I want to scream that I don't "like" people:

I consume people. I scheme to slip into their skins,
put a thumb to my pulse and feel ten hearts beating.

So, no, I don't desire my girlfriend's best friend
except to zip into his flesh, Hannibal Lecter-esque,

and wear him out; down; into submission; forever and ever
until I get bored (so, maybe a month).

I have always craved people
though I controlled it better in my anorexic days.

The doctor says that's evolutionary: when you're starving
you don't have the time (or natural lubricant) for sex

and it's true that for years I was blameless as Clorox,
was my own haughty halo of righteousness.

I remember when I was still a virgin
somebody told me that sex smelled like Thai food

and I thought, *how repulsive!*, and now I think
lustily of slurping noodles and spring rolls and ass holes.

I'm so expansive my skinny pants don't fit
(it's almost as if my body were never that manageable)

(as if my wants were never so meek) (as if my whole world
couldn't once fit in a half-empty grocery basket

dangling from my brittle wrist:
a universe of baby carrots and skim milk).

I used to shop only for my next meal because I didn't dare take
                                                        up space—
not even in my own refrigerator.

One reckless night I broke down and ate
a whole box of cereal I didn't even like

though I loved the ensuing punishment:
pacing the neighborhood from midnight to dawn, full

of calculations: how far to escape
my own tastes,

how much a girl had to burn
to become something

better. What I'm trying to say is, I wanted so wickedly
to be wantless; I aspired to a purity unknown to this world;

48 ♀ Sinister Wisdom 112- *Moon and Cormorant*

I lived inside the blazing white
margins of my own life;

I learned there was nothing so lonely
as being my own role model.

Now I'm a revolving door of modeling: at work
donning Talbots pants, same as my mother did (how to admit

that I've never felt closer to her
than in an Eddie Bauer blouse and low-heeled shoe);

at home cinching myself into pajama pants
handed down from my girlfriend's Nana;

or my girlfriend's old sandals, the ones crusted with dirt;
or the black leather strap-on we bought at Rick's Toy Box.

If I could, I'd wake as someone new every day,
raid her kitchen cabinet and measure his waist,

flex her biceps in the mirror and trail his tongue
over the bend in his elbow, wondering if with taste

comes understanding. I want everyone, which no one wants
to hear, especially not my girlfriend.

As if I weren't flighty enough—I'm hundred-hungered, needy
in a way I've never divulged outside of therapy

(what if I'm incapable of settling down?)
(what if my desires are always almost expired?)

(what if I stopped lying to everybody
and admitted that I only want guys

when I'm with girls, girls when I'm with guys?)
(what if I corralled everybody who's ever penetrated me

and admitted that I didn't cum, didn't come close
because I needed it bigger

and by bigger I mean larger than life
and by it I mean existence?)

I need a whole pile of people who'll let me
slide behind their eyes and judge humanity anew.

"Am I even gay?"—But how can I be
whittled down to anything so concrete?

What I am: soft for your earwax and bunions,
your kneecaps and lungs. Lend me your body, let me eat.

ON OUR WEDDING

Julie Weiss

For Olga (April 12, 2013)

I wake to a symphony of Valdeluz winds
playing a ballad against our window pane.
Below, the patio trees are whirling,
embraced in mid-dance, breathless, in love.
Our pink walls have turned a shade hotter,
like the flush in my face
your smile kindled that winter
when you walked up the stairs,
into Plaza de Chueca
and kissed my cheeks for the first time.

Because of you, life has taken on new splendor.

This is what I'm thinking
as I lay my hand on your thigh
and you cover it with your own.
I am dazzled by the ordinary.
You dip a cookie into cocoa, I crunch cereal—
same old scraping chairs and clinking plates,
dismal newscasts and morning yawns,
all of it brimming with extraordinary beauty.

Dazzled by our matching gold bands,
the way they glitter like planetary rings.
I tell you, each of us is a sphere
around which the other has settled into orbit.

When I said "I do"
and signed my name next to yours,
I meant: whatever rogue forces in the world
may spin us out of control
I'll always come full circle,
back to the burning in my heart.

I meant, from now on, there's only this:
dawn sky cracking open,
sunlight spilling through blinds
like the birth of some marvelous winged creature
poised to take flight

and I kiss you as if saying
hold on tight, let's ride together,
for better or for worse,
all the days of our lives.

DANCING WITH YOU

Marisa Crane

is like dreaming in reverse.
    Fearless, I rise from reality and soar

on the serene wings of
    my subconscious, and it is

medicinal, a delicious freedom
even pineapple kush fails to grant.

Dancing with you is like swallowing
a moonbeam, like meeting a group

of aliens and learning more about myself
than I do about them. It is eleven thirty

and we are drifting through
    the night's modest motivation, crowned,

if only by our own standards of beauty.
    Dancing with you is like

licking the soft underbelly of a god.
    If that is offensive, need I remind

the gods that hubris is not a punishable
offense if they cannot capture us.

Dancing with you is like dissolving the
    bleak restraints of life, like twisting

tongues in dark, sagacious basements,
    like the acquisition of love prior to needing it.

LAST KISS

Chanice Cruz

The last time I kissed my mother she didn't tell me she was gone,
it was the last time *Home* coiled itself around my body,
somehow, her stiffness felt so alive under the right side of my face,
ears, once only worn for finding her heart beat.

There was a chill in the air the day of her funeral,
it was June,

the last time I kissed my mother, nobody looked into her eyelids,
everyone bought tears in their pockets, the salt room, burned my
                                                                    eyes,
nobody wanted to touch her but forced themselves to anyway.

My thumb outlined the outside of her collarbone,
palms washed away all of the nervous fingers from her skin;
some wishing it was someone else and others thankful it wasn't
                                                                    them.
I traced her soaked cheeks, their thoughts ripping through the tips
                                                                    of me,
I couldn't feel her anymore, wiping so many lips left printed with
                                                    the back of my hand.

I kissed my mother for the last time,
every filled hole now drained from my body,
they all made sure to hug me afterwards,
hands like rose-thorns scratching my back,
I still carry ghost scars everywhere I go.

when I kissed my mother, it was our last moment together,
the last memory, my Latina Snow White with no way of waking up,
I never look back, eyes always away from who we used to be.

HOW TO BE EATEN BY A BUTTERFLY

Chanice Cruz

Become vulnerable without apology, there is no
use for cover-ups, masks, the poker-face, do not
flinch when skinny legs land on your upper-thigh,
I know your're squeamish against such fragile things,
but be stone stomach, clear throat, no need for
vomiting now.

Lay under your memories, try to think beautiful,
as she starts to pick little clumps of your flesh and
stuff it into her mouth, let her be gluttony; remember
your mother's best smiles, put them into categories,
it will take a while.

It has been three hours when the butterfly invites
her friends over to the festival of your body, do not
tense, as they pick at pieces that have never been
whole, touched, loved. Think your mother's death
how friends came to cry with you, when your ex-
girlfriend drove miles to kiss you; do not let them
take your lips, clenched, your body was a sky rocket,
afterwards you hid your mouth knew it was ONLY a
kiss to her so why want more?

Those are things you only admit to your notebook.

There is a rabble of butterflies eating away at the
"Natalie" of your chest, it is a matter of hours before
they squeeze themselves between rib bones and find
your heart. Be patience, it is all over soon, look for your
sister in the clouds, her thunderbolt mouth, the way she

wore "the child's honesty", remember how right you feel
as she hugs you, believe the armor picking at you is just
her presence, and go with your mother,

peacefully.

BUDDING 1

Emel Karakozak

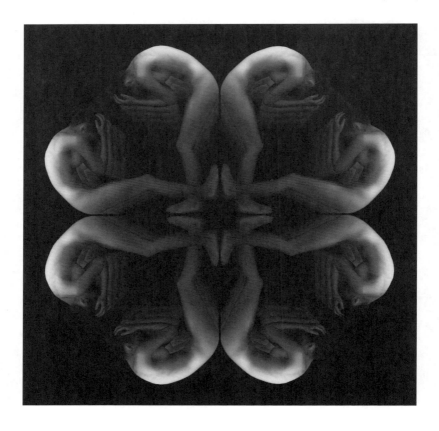

BUDDING 2

Emel Karakozak

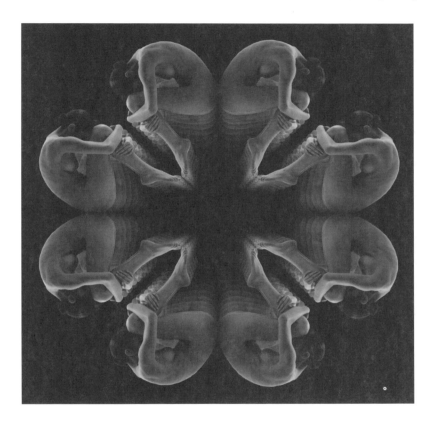

BUDDING 5

Emel Karakozak

BUDDING 7
Emel Karakozak

BUDDING 9

Emel Karakozak

BUDDING 10

Emel Karakozak

BUDDING 11

Emel Karakozak

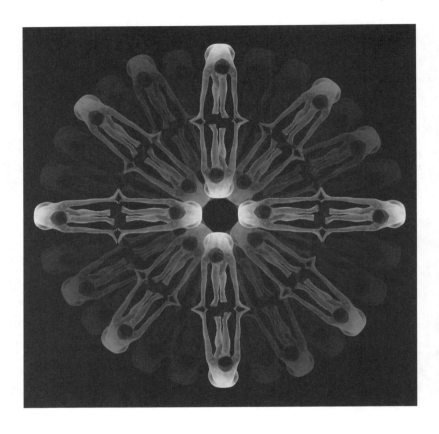

BUDDING 12

Emel Karakozak

BUDDING 13

Emel Karakozak

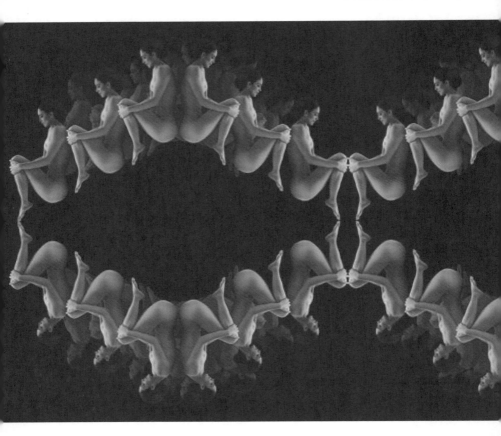

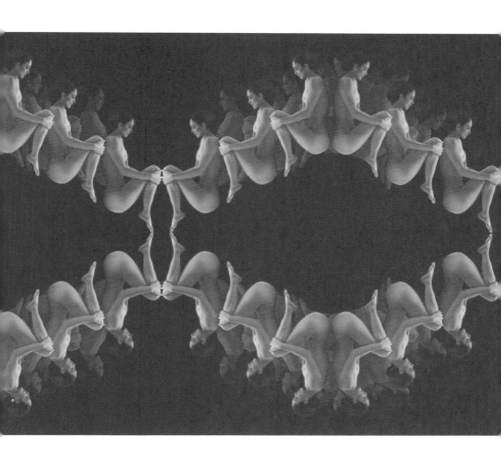

BUDDING 14

Emel Karakozak

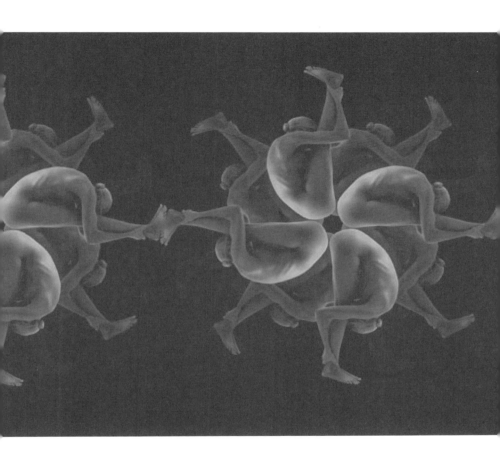

BUDDING 16

Emel Karakozak

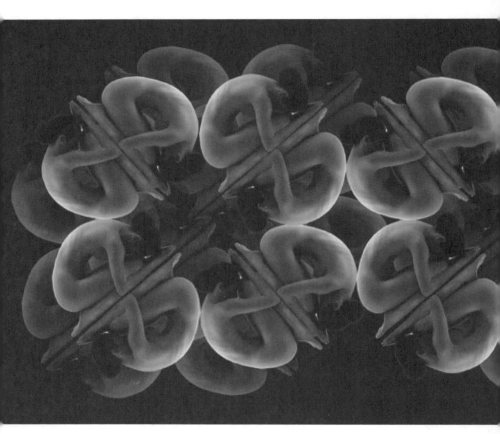

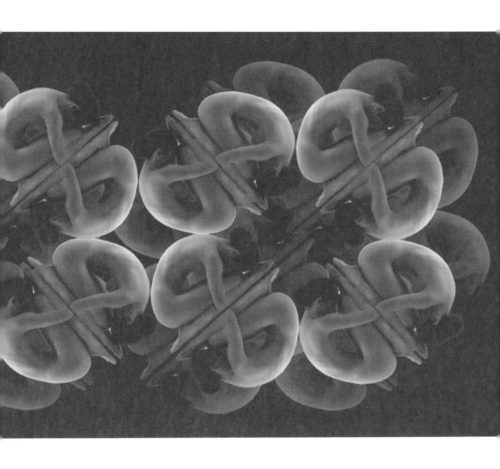

ARTIST STATEMENT

Emel Karakozak

BUDDING

Woman is very similar to nature in birth-giving and life-blooming characteristics. Many languages use the term of 'mother nature' while referring to nature. Woman is the bridge, able to recreate herself and the source. Woman not only causes a miracle by giving birth, but also has the ability to reconstitute herself spiritually. She fulfills this by putting herself into the center.

In the exhibition 'Budding,' Emel Karakozak depicts these characteristics of woman using all the aesthetic and composition figures of photography. Though the word 'budding' reminds us of the 'body' in English, it means 'reproduction, regain of life, regeneration of a cell', just like the photography of Karakozak.

I THINK I'M IN LOVE WITH YOU
BUT PLEASE DON'T TELL

Lila Tziona

every time I think I've forgotten you
you dye your hair or wear that shirt or smile
and I'm reminded that you are still
an ever-present demon in my mind

I find myself looking at photos of you
like it's all I have to live for
like you're all I have to live for
and yet here we are
I'm still dead
and you're not mine

I wonder if your hair is as silky as it looks
I wonder if I'll love your voice more when I hear it say
my name the way I say yours
do you ever think about me?
is my face imprinted behind yours, the way yours is etched into
my brain like a tombstone crumbling in an abandoned graveyard
are the footprints in the soil above my rotting body yours?

I doodled your eyes on the back of my homework
and missed the entire lesson
and even when that test came back with a C
I could only laugh
because your name starts with a C
and it was almost perfect, wasn't it?

and each time I feel like you're gone from my soul
I see that perfect smile and I know we'll be old and gray before
I stop thinking about you and I'll only stop when old age takes

away my memories with my joints and health. I'll imagine I see
 you reflected in the eyes of my children and grandchildren
a replica of who we were when we were young
but I'm just an empty shell waiting to be filled by you
and you're tired of boxes with nothing inside so you pass over
me every single time
and so we keep building prototypes of what we want
mine all look like you
and yours have nothing to do with me

"if you could make anyone in the world want you,
would you?" the question was posed to me
and I didn't even hesitate
your face filled my sight
you were all I could see
and the answer
of course
was yes
if I could make you want me,
there'd be nothing else I'd ever need
"wouldn't you have regrets? wouldn't you worry you chose
wrong?" but if I could make you want me
like I want you
I know there'd be no other choice

you remind me of the stained glass windows in the church
I was in once during a wedding
it was the first time I had ever been in a church
and I lost track of time while examining the stories
they were intricate and beautiful
like you
but they distracted me and I forgot where I was
and I lost myself in the opaque colors and the filtered light

and by the time I was done looking at them
the wedding was over
and I was tired

she figured out it was you, she said,
because when you were in the room
you were all I could see
and apparently it wasn't subtle
apparently the way my eyes follow you
and my words disappear
my soul is hollowed out
and my shadow stretches towards you
apparently all of that is very noticeable
cause she figured out it was you

and my eyes grow tired from looking into the light
and my eyelids long to close and block the world out
and I let them because looking at you is too painful
I wonder if it would hurt more knowing your eyes were wide open
or knowing they were closed too
just like mine

it doesn't matter
because you deserve better
I can only offer you scars underneath a baggy sweatshirt
and goosebumps on exposed legs
even during the winter (because the cold makes me return to my body
but it leaves me with a chill)
and a gnawing ache in my chest I get every time I
think I've forgotten you

OF PRAYERS

Kaye Lin Kuphal

Exultation, invocation, imploration, at times adoration, the prayer is a spiritual communication, a supplication in which the mortal and the maligned beseech the greater beings to grant strength, beauty, and deliverance. The prayer is a humble petition to the powers that be. The prayer is random, ritual, continuous. Precor, precari, precatus sum. We are nothing but particles of sand in a desert, and the desert is vast, and the desert is empty. But, in the desert, we can find ourselves in the oases in the sands, in petals of bush flowers, in succulent fruits and kit foxes and the tiny horned reptiles that wrestle under the rocks. Something in nothing. Nothing is something. We pray for perspicacity, for sensitivity, for vision. We know that something must be scaling up the sweltering air and that sometimes we require assistance in opening our eyes. We need—gods—perhaps human, perhaps celestial, perhaps historical, perhaps abstract. We need an object of belief to produce a new strange power within us, we dare not believe we ourselves have the power, we have been attempting and attempting and failing and failing; we need something to blame and something to glorify, something to guilt us and something to gift us ourselves and our reality. Heaven is the way to earth, and earth is everything we do not trust we know.

When I pray, I roll my lips around my double reed, freshly scraped on all the essential planes and edges, press down the suitable keys, and make my instrument advocate for me with all the elegance my body stumbles over otherwise. I took up the oboe because as a solo piano player, I wanted to play music with other people; because I was incapable of playing the flute; and because a girl I admired also played the oboe. She was red lipped and blonde haired and superb at singing and writing. Naturally, I wanted to have more in common with her. So, I opened my hands to the oboe I playfully named Mellifluous, later succeeded by Sonorous, and I named every reed so that they had "C" names: Caliginous, Charisma, Chrysanthemum, Calliope. Back then, I purchased already finished reeds and hoped they would last more than a month. I took care not to break them against my teeth and give each enough time to be broken in for the sake of good music. After practice and performance, back into their little cases they went, so snug between Styrofoam and plastic they could be inside miniature coffins. Every aspect of the art of playing mattered to me: if my instrument screws were turned to just the right degree, if I had polished my keys recently enough, if I could get the bubbles out from under my pads immediately after I heard them. Band was fine and fair for friendships, orchestra was fine and fair for musical literature, but I still did not sing the way I needed to truly feel otherness that I discovered later.

After entering college, chamber music became my particular prayer. A couple times a week, I met with a few other people, and we played off each other, eyes catching eyes and notes catching up with other notes, the harpsichord and cellos keeping the rhythmic bass, and the violin, viola, and my own soprano voice passing the melodies between each other, ornate Baroque runs and sixteenth note phrases for measures onward, a race we had to remind ourselves to slow down—slow down—enjoy. I am known to dance when I play. As a woodwind player, I work especially from my diaphragm, but also, I bounce on my feet, flex my abdomen, weave my head, raise and lower my shoulders according to the musical dynamics. In my first chamber group, I was stiffer, quieter, more uncertain about asking for time in my longer phrases. I did not know which to match, the cello, the violin, or the viola, or how important it was to listen to the breaths of each player. Years later and several performances having developed me, at my last concert, I stood on stage with visiting Bolivian musicians and most of my college's chamber players, and I felt the dance as never before—here the drums and here the flute, here the violins and here the guitars, here the theme leaping between us, the repetition and clapping and yearning, yearning, asking the audience to take pleasure in a piece of beauty with us. There was a language barrier; the visiting musicians spoke only Spanish, and the rest of us were able to say a few words back at best. In playing the music together though, we understood what we collectively wanted: to make people dance, to make people move, to bring everyone together.

The music inhabits me, and I want only to understand what it is trying to say to me, talking back to it with all my air, all my body, because when I play, when I pray, I feel closer to whatever numina are still captured in the air. If my sound is just right, my vibrato even, my decays measured, my pitch pure, I release the spirits, they release me, and for those moments, I thrum. Because of music, I know how to communicate when the words escape me, from my own reluctance and anxiety or from not knowing how to speak the language of an acquaintance. Music is a personal as well as common prayer, not limited only to those who can manipulate the art itself, but also for the girl dancing to the beats breaking through her speakers, for the boy jamming his earphones on for his walk through the streets, for the child learning their first lullabies from the throats of their mother. They are praying, they are desiring, they are touching joy, fear, grief, godliness. We talk to each other and to our souls when we put the sounds together and find the meanings among their acoustic distances.

Prayer is the sound, the raging howl, the word. In this magnetic field of purposeful communication, the lilt of language, the pause of punctuation, the way lines and curves are interpreted are the shapers of cosmos. Language has a different grammar than music, but all the same, it is a way we offer our wishes up to the great powers. We write to each other, to our past and future selves, to our gods asking if they are listening, if they are reading, if they will give our thoughts new life on the page. Perhaps reality is exactly what it is, but is it not true that there is the universe, there is what we see of it, and there is what we translate of our perceptions— and we inevitably live according to what we imagine to be. Such is the nature of action based on perception. Even as we write, sometimes the prayer is unclear, and I often cannot discern what I was trying to tell myself in a poem after waking to find I really did finish something as I fell into the abyss of time between midnight and morning. The shape of my language is images and sounds, pitch and pace and flow and rhythm, words that are meant to be said and savored. I wish that I were a bit more coherent, a bit more direct, but I am hoping to find my way into meaning all the same. We are all writing for understanding, for freshness, for getting deeper inside our existence. We write new worlds, past lives, particular magics into being, and we ask the universe for them even if they may live on the page only. Give a little of our lives, and we might get a little life back. This is what we pray, anyhow, that is what we pray, word by word, phoneme by phoneme.

When we thought the world was flat, we were cautious of the edge of the horizon, sailed our ships slightly this other way so that we did not sink like the hot sun into the depths of darkness. Now we understand the universe—so we think—and we consider how we should conduct ourselves based on the conjectures, string theory, multiverse, loop quantum gravity, whatever else vies to be the grand unifying theory of science. We say, this is it, and we find that it is not, and we say something new after a few more thoughts, hoping that maybe this time, we found the right words for what we are living. There are theorems, and there are proofs, and there is the mystery of ourselves that we attempt to uncover. We see the shadows scrawled across our walls and leaves and grasses, the curious pulsing arteries, the changes in colors as chemical reactions progress across galaxies and memories and faces, and we probe the mystery, striving to control and account for the variables, collecting our spectra, analyzing our data, and offering up our understandings to the universe to reject or accept us as it will.

Thus, I strive in the labs I have worked in to comprehend the chemistry of existence and how certain signals surge above the noise. So far, I have been more measurer than maker in the field of research, conducting spectroscopy after spectroscopy to correlate the shapes of the resulting graphs to electronic properties that must be causing these specific interactions. All the same, I know where my data and elucidations fit into the scheme of science as I talk to other students who engage in biophysics and inorganic chemistry and organic synthesis and physical chemistry research. We work to answer how cells maintain their health by regulation of autophagy, what ligands induce the most desirable properties when bonded to metal centers, when a chemical probe for diseases can be considered successful, why the atmosphere around us has such a profound effect on the life on Earth. The answers are not easy, the technology is never quite advanced enough or our brains developed enough to understand what we are gathering up number by number, but we make our attempts, our prayers that we can understand how we are here and how we might remain.

But, these are only a couple of the more obvious examples of prayer. Prayer is throwing a disk, boiling a soup, walking through willows, chasing after a passing friend. Prayer is color and etching and rowing and weeping. Prayer is laughter and recitation and sleeping and fantasizing. Prayer is living, is striving, is holding back in anticipation of how the world might bite back. Prayer is clutching hope until it is white with its impending disappearance, is deciding to leave the worn path and take chances under the darkening canopy of low-rising trees. Prayer is what the soul cries out when it is ascending, when it is diminishing, when it is stressed, when it is jubilant. Prayer is lying across another's lap during the darker morning with bits of memory sloughing off shiny honest faces. Prayer is arriving at the only open ice cream shop a few minutes before their closing and asking for a double fudge sundae with the too sweet cherry, asking forgiveness for being here and for needing that sweetness. Prayer is talking about the rarity of good mangoes with other mango lovers in the middle of New York when that good fruit and rice and sugar are why many of us are here post-colonization, standing on land not-so-many-greats-grandparents worked over for little to no pay for European nations' staples. Prayer is the lover herself, agape with all her graces spilling out of her mouth, showing off her new muscles with all the subtlety of a ship sending fireworks off its decks, pointing to the plush animal she has waiting for you when you finally come home.

Prayer, like life, can be a darker thing. I pray on occasion with a knife to the wrists, with a hammer to the thighs, with the rubbing open of raised old scars. I wish for a sooner end than seems to be in sight. My prayer is then less about joy and connection and more about hissing out my hurt in every way possible. My prayer is spiteful, is selfish, is violent, is watchful for the smallest answer to help me decide how to handle myself today. Is it—to God—or to myself—or to the universe? All I know is I ask and ask and ask what now should I do with myself. Prayer can be ultimate, bodily, personal, despairing. Prayer can be sleeping with someone you barely know when you have finally begun a relationship with the partner you have wanted for years. Prayer can be demanding secrecy for a disastrous truth. Prayer can be the last breath from a now-decaying body, the soul but a small sphere destined to dissipate into air, and the universe eats it up like it is the tastiest morsel that has ever been sacrificed to it.

My favorite prayer has always been the relationship. If language is the mediator between meaning and sound, then the relationship is the mediator between self and other. Simple, somewhat crass in its logic, but such is the crux of compassion and understanding. Ask me who my friends are, and I eagerly open up, for these are the people whose lives I consider when asked how I myself am doing. How can I but match myself against those who have taken lodging within my heart? At 11:11,

I cross my fingers and think my prayer to the powers that be, to make happy and healthy the people I consider my own: Hayley Brandy Leo Nghi Krislynn Lillian Matthew Cassie Jasmine Jessica Travis Zaarah Logan Haley Marina Soumya Cynthia Emily Žana Maurice Kevin Pomaa Mezmur Quan Hope Richel Alyson Christian Aleah Hannah Brittany Michael Landon Romelia Tiffany Will Elie Virginia Frehley Alex Leslie Henry. These people have invaded my introversion and demanded my attention in the gentlest, sweetest manner possible. They call me cinnamon roll and bibingka and soulmate and penguin, show me their hand-felted shells and fat cats and stickers of shibas in bushes. In turn, I call them dearheart and sweeting and beloved, send them musical improvisation videos and personal poems and reminders to sleep, to eat, to tell me if they need anything that I might provide. I adore them for being the people who can maybe get this life right, who deserve it even if I do not. And so, I am thankful, and I put them before me, and I ask again and again if I can do more, if my prayer is sincere enough for this relationship to work out.

I met my partner Krislynn when I was eighteen and had recently broken up with my first local girlfriend. Krislynn, from afar in Washington state, had liked my pictures on a blog site, and I decided to feel out her interest in me. We talked about homemade focaccia and Debussy and microbiology and family, about being overly friendly with strangers and the difficulty of coming out to our families, about how we might fit our lives together despite her living in Washington and my living in Kentucky at the time. She lived in Hawaii and I in New York when I attended undergraduate college, five or six hours apart in time zones depending on daylight savings, but we called, we texted, we found time to nap together and stress together and gossip together. Sometimes I am terrible and mad and sad, and we fight about my isolation and refusal to talk all that often with her even when I let my friends in, because romantic relationships are so much more expectation and effort. These are the worst during my depressive bouts. I let her see my beating upon my head and chest and thighs, and I ask her to kill me, for I cannot figure it out on my own. I know this is not the thing to ask other people, particularly those who love you, but rather this is brash and manipulative and unforgivable. Still, I cannot help myself when all I want is for her to stop asking so much of me and instead let me go. Is this spiteful more than honest? I do not know. I am working on being alone and not lashing out, for I know I am as desperate and despicable as I feel myself to be. The love and care and frustration are a prayer as much as the small implicit understandings between people. Caring is the prayer that people are worth having and saving, the prayer that we are meaningful mistakes, the prayer that even if nothing is true, I love the lie of these people. Perhaps they love the lie of me, too. I pray I can be better than the lie, better than the truth, better than whoever I have been and likely should be. Maybe there are medicines or therapy for it. God, I pray they work.

Sometimes, it is easier than all that, just a moment, a night Hope, Leo, and I shared when he came back for the weekend from researching at NIH. We started by meeting up in the college bookstore, where I commented on how much skinnier he had gotten, and then we headed to grub on American Chinese food from Main Moon. Energized by their company and wanting to keep the flavors of food and laughter coming, I led us to get ciders from the sandwich shop and plastic-wrapped chipwiches, brownie and original, from the dairy store. We walked down the street back to the upperclassmen housing, chatting about nothing that mattered, and stopped by Leslie's house before heading to my apartment. My roommate Pomaa was awake and home, and we sat around each other and watched *Hercules* before calling off the night. To be young and physically capable and in company with each other and able to trap time, even for just a night, it was one of the purest and simplest prayers I might have ever made.

Prayer is a personal matter. We can pray together, but what is said and what is intended will always be known only to each person.

Prayer is spectacle and sullen solitude and symphony and stunted structure. Prayer is beauty and meaning and truth and lie. Prayer is fracture and decay and living. Prayer is my 11:11 wish for health and happiness for all. Prayer is staring at the clock as it screeches past 4:37 a.m. When we wish, when we need, when we live, prayer is put forth, and the universe answers as it will. Is it useful? Does it change the laws of the universe? Does it matter whether you have wished for something in spite or wished for something just too predictable? The terrible thing is that if it is useful or if it is not, it is inevitable, every person prays in their own or collectively organized way.

The prayer is the soul's desperation to enact change with that energy contained within matter. Open your heart, let the soul free, and let the singing sweep out like rings on disturbed water. We are children, skipping our stones, fascinated by what happens to the waters of our lives. The prayer is what brings people together, to each other, to the world in which they might exist. We must pray because how else might we gain the ability to encompass our conflicting beliefs and perhaps gain their resolution? We pray to channel the music, to make the mind clever, to open ourselves to whatever understandings are scattered across our skies. The prayer is our admission that we need help, that we do not need help, that something is beautiful and painful and necessary. Prayer is a plea, and we all beg a little at some point to figure out what is in this air around us. Open up, breathe out, let the prayer free. It might be answered, it might not, but we have to make our hopes and confusions known or we will always wonder: What if we had simply asked, had simply made evident our pleasure or pain, rather than utterly give up without asking the powers that be to provide more or less or the same.

LAVENDER BLACK

Yeva Johnson

With gratitude to James Baldwin, Audre Lorde, and June Jordan

I am not your Negro

I am not your black lesbian unicorn
    I am not your
family doctor, nor am I
    your muse.

I was born a negro,
    transmogrified through
        decades to
            Black, African-American

    And now back to black.

I am not your big girl
    I am not your girl, nor your woman
        No damsel in distress.

I am not your
    Only Jew
        You can't identify me by
            my yarmulke because
                I don't wear one.

I am not happy to be part
    Of one of the most racist
        religions in America
Because, I am not your
    Unitarian Universalist.

I am not your
        Queer person of color
                Advocate

Who recognizes crimes
        and misdemeanors
                on sight.

No need to wait for
        years of evidence
                to build up

To the inevitable
        recognition of the need
for impeachment.

I am not your
        classical musician
                dabbling in the house
                        of jazz.

I am not your elder
        aging, crone
                now aching in the
                        joints.

I am not yours

I just am.

A CASTE RELEASED OFFERS SOME TIME IN CONTEMPLATION

Yeva Johnson

For Phyllis

Radiant sun warms
All creatures, equally- no need to
Distinguish, create hierarchies or
Incite violence or hatred.
Capable of supplying the necessary energy for
All life forms on the planet,
Leaving no leaf unturned, no one

Left-out, far-flung.
Expansive view includes
Surprising absence of castes or dichotomies only
Beings loving and trusting other beings,
Instruments for the greater good.
Annotations to histories long forgotten creates a
Nexus between the real and the possible.

Frame a new global perspective
Encompassing love in myriad forms.
Mend hearts, create pathways
Indicative of human possibility, open up and
Never lose sight of where we've tread,
Including the painful stories and
Secrets, now exposed to light and air.
Time to take stock and declare: we are here.

CODA TO A ROMANTIC INTERLUDE

Yeva Johnson

Mirrored spaces befuddle as
my hand reaches
grasping for love, not
shards of glass
sprinkled over digits cringing.
Is there no
Real love?

Is there no
Real woman
whose juices flowed
when we were together?
Were they just my own
imaginings?

Hot, heavy
pronouncements of
love disintegrate on a
wind of propriety.
I refuse to be
the secret lover,

so I just dry
up, disappear
and keep my bleeding
hands to myself.

POETIC SISTERS

Yeva Johnson

Her last poem
slips away. My fingertips
close The Book of
Complete Works
and I miss her.
I yearn for her
despite not yet
having put her book
in its rightful
place on my shelf.

So when I turn to my other
sister outsider,
I can't yet give my self
up to Audre
because Pat
Parker beckons
me still with
her innards.

As I had to
with June Jordan,
I learn that I
must live without
her. All that's
left are Pat's pages.

After I recover my
more even keeled, black
lesbian, mother, pacifist, Jewish

feminist physician self,
then I can drink Audre in.
Drink deep but slow
like sampling a fine wine.
Lorde caught me up completely
in the poem for Martha.

I'm hooked,
sinking and swimming
reading and rejoicing
and mourning simultaneously.
Oh sister outsiders
would that I had seen you
Alive!

SINISTER WISDOM SAYS HELLO

Yeva Johnson

Reaching my digital
finger
Into the universe
Calling, calling.
Jewish Lesbians
echo back
and this time
Multiethnic
maybe multinational.
I answer
the call
Yes, yes
Hineni, Hineni
Black, queer, poet
musician, humanistic
fat, pacifist,
mother, feminist
I too was at
Sinai.

CATHERINE NICHOLSON AND *SINISTER WISDOM*
Winifred D. Cherry

Editor's Note: At the time of her death, Winifred D. Cherry was working on a profile of Catherine Nicholson (one of the founding editors of *Sinister Wisdom*). She did not have time to complete this project but left behind this manuscript, which has been lightly edited. *Sinister Wisdom* is grateful to Cherry's spouse, Elizabeth Edmiston, for permission to publish this piece.

Catherine Nicholson is the only person I know who when she first opens a book, looks to see who published the work before glancing through it. Old habits are hard to break. As a former editor of *Sinister Wisdom*, a periodical devoted to discussing issues central to the lesbian community, Catherine Nicholson is very aware of the important role publishers play in getting an author's word to readers. I spoke with Nicholson several times during the summer and fall of 1997. Here I present a look at the world of lesbian publishing Nicholson was very much a part of in the 1970s and the broader world of the lesbian feminist movement which publishers like Nicholson helped make possible by giving radical thinkers a place in which to raise issues and voice concerns. This piece weaves comments made by Nicholson prior to her death (in italics) together with statements made in the years in which Nicholson was one of the women at the forefront of lesbian publishing in the 1970s.

Catherine Nicholson was born in Troy, North Carolina. She received her Ph.D. at Northwestern and taught theatre for many years at the University of North Carolina at Charlotte. Along with her partner Harriet Desmoines, Nicholson began *Sinister Wisdom*, the longest running periodical devoted to lesbian issues.

Coming on the heels of the second wave of feminism and the Stonewall riots, the 1970s saw the rise of the lesbian feminist movement. Some lesbian feminists chose to control their own language and to debate the issues in their own forums. Thus in the 1970s, there were several publications that emerged devoted to lesbian theory. Though much of the debate over issues raised in the movement took place in Washington DC, New York, and other northern cosmopolitan centers, there was a radical voice that emerged in the South as well.

CN: *"The most radical thinking about who lesbians were and what their mission was actually took place in the '70's. You got it from the Furies in Washington... What they really wanted to do was change the world and they wanted to do things for women. This was definitely feminist. They wanted to overthrow all patriarchal rights. Within the women's movement, the lesbians were the most radical and the serious lesbian feminists considered themselves the leaders, in a sense, of the women's movement, the feminist movement. Lesbians, in a sense, could think farther and think more because they actually didn't have to do things for men.*

Well, of course, there were a lot of women who were just trying to get Equal Rights and we had no use for them, you know. Who wanted to be equal to men? We grow up in a patriarchal world and so all of us had been infected and we had the imprinting in us. We called it 'the prick in the head'. When we started the magazine, it was saying to people, "you know, you have to think."

We attacked humanism, too, liberal humanism. All their articles used just "man". They'd say that it meant women, of course. The publishers of the Humanist Quarterly *couldn't bring themselves to recognize the feminist movement. Now they absolutely deplored racism and they used these terms that were very strong and when they finally said something about feminists, they said it in a much milder way. They were strongly not getting it. After a while they did. We were attacking them straight on. People were just appalled. I mean humanism, that's the greatest thing.*

We were examining everything, every idea, every concept. So that's what was so exiting about it. Someone asked Harriet what feminism did for her. "It really gave me back my mind," she said. And it is true.

So that's where it was in the '70s and as far as lesbians were concerned. We thought we were dealing with everything. We are accused now of trying to wipe out sexuality and all that. Well, actually we didn't play it up. Most of the lesbian books that had been written before, sex was very important in them and being involved sexually with a woman was about the only definition for a lesbian. So we were saying that lesbians were more than that.

We were trying to get our history together. We tried to rediscover lesbians who had been wiped out. I was especially interested in Jane Ellen Harrison, for instance, back when I was doing my dissertation on Greek tragedy. Harrison actually did research and tore apart the classical myths and ripped them to pieces. You can find the traditional view of the Olympians, which is a patriarchal view, at the corner drugstore. Harrison's was a completely different view of all the these. She went back to what they came from. She became a threat to traditional interpretation because she showed where these goddesses came from. She had no respect for the Olympians at all. That's why she got wiped out.

In the mid 1970's Catherine Nicholson and her partner Harriet Desmoines were looking for a way to support the movement. Both were interested in publishing and decided to put their efforts toward an outlet for lesbian feminist concerns. Together they founded *Sinister Wisdom*.

CN: We both loved the Amazon Quarterly *(which had recently stopped publishing.) We definitely wanted to do something with writing and publishing and we talked to June Arnold and she said, "Why don't you start your own? We think you should do something where you are. So we talked about it and decided that we would continue* Amazon Quarterly *but we would have to start a new thing to do it. So that is what we did.*

We started on it in December of 1975 and the first issue came out in July of 1976 on the 200th anniversary of the Declaration of Independence, a very appropriate time, don't you think?

Where does the title *Sinister Wisdom* come from?

CN: *Harriet and I just loved the phrase. It comes from Joanna Russ'* The Female Man. *In the story an older woman who had come from another planet fell in love with a younger girl and one of the things she asked when she was attracted to this girl was, 'should I tamper with her . . . is this sinister wisdom that I am bringing to this?" It was about a relationship between an older and a younger woman and that was our relationship. We named it this way because it is from the left and the right is a patriarchal view.*

What is the meaning of the logo?

In the first issue of the journal, Catherine and Harriet wrote: The logo comes from Jane Ellen Harrison's *Prologomena to the Study of Greek Religion*, a Boeotian plate painting of the corn goddess Demeter and Persephone in one figure.

CN: *"Prologomena" actually means "before the word itself, before civilization in a sense, before 5th century tragedy."*

Catherine Nicholson and Harriet Desmoines published *Sinister Wisdom* from 1976-1981. They began with three issues in 1976-77. Subscription rate was $4.50 for one year. In the fifteenth year of the publication, publishers took a look back at the history of *Sinister Wisdom*. In that issue Nicholson explains exactly how the periodical came to be.

In the Fifteenth Anniversary retrospective edition, they wrote: We made a flyer and sent it to women and institutions whose addresses were published in the *New Woman's Survival Sourcebook*, to Beth Hodges who had edited a special issue in *Margins* on "Lesbian Feminist Writing and Publishing" (1974), and to anyone who we could think of that might be interested in contributing or subscribing.

94 ♀ Sinister Wisdom 112- *Moon and Cormorant*

The early issues were typed on a rented IBM Selectric and pasted up by hand with tips from Laurel Galana's "How to Make a Magazine." One thousand copies of the first issue were printed for $450.00 by an old family firm in Clover, South Carolina that printed Baptist church literature. The owner of the press did much of the work himself to avoid letting his female staff see the work and be shocked by the content. Volunteers had to collate and staple pages themselves. At the first collating party, volunteers worked to the music of Alix Dobkin, Meg Christian, and Nina Simone.

In April of 1976 Nicholson shares her nervousness about the first issue with the readers: I'm thrilled by its integrity of vision . . . but I'm scared to death by the bold admission that we are lesbians - that *Sinister Wisdom* is devoted to the creation of a lesbian imagination, "and in all known societies lesbians are a criminal class, those who are cast out." To declare these things in print! One the other hand, announcing around, above, under, and through the truth of who we are and what we aim to do seems to me unthinkable. Coming from a career of doing the impossible in theatre, I was more confident about the doing, but coming from a life of disguising, encoding, I was mortally afraid of telling the truth about myself and my vision.

Who read *Sinister Wisdom?*

CN: *A few men bought it and a number of straight women. We didn't mind and they subscribed to it and we thought that after all they might learn something and that was the whole point.*

In August of 1976, Nicholson and Desmoines and the members of the Charlotte Lesbian Press Collective drove to Nebraska to attend the first history making Women in Print Conference where they met with other women involved in all aspect of publishing. In the fall of 1976, the actual printing of *Sinister Wisdom* relocated to Whole Women Press in Durham, NC. "The Lady," as they affectionately called it, would now be in the "gentle, caring hands of lesbian printers" (Fifteenth Anniversary Edition 325).

Spring 2019 ♀ 95

After the publication of the sixth issue, the entire operation moved to Lincoln, Nebraska in 1978. *Sinister Wisdom* also went to four issues a year. In 1979, Nicholson and Desmoines shifted their focus from actually producing the magazine to ensuring its continuation. In 1981 Adrienne Rich and Michelle Cliff took on the editorship of the magazine.

What happened to the lesbian feminist movement in the 80s and 90s and early 00s?

CN: It's not popular anymore. It's considered passé these days. It hasn't died out. I'm still a lesbian but it is very shocking to me that a group of lesbians today may not be feminists. I was with a group of lesbian once and in our discussion I realized that there weren't any feminists in the room. They were lesbians but not feminists. They were saying that things can't be changed. There is nothing that can be changed. I don't see too many activists today. I don't see a lot of activism out there.

I'm certainly not the radical. I have realized that there was a stage that our revolution got through but I think it's necessary. If you say those things today, no effect at all. When I go back to the first issue of Sinister Wisdom, I am appalled. What in the world? It was so polemical. I know what we were thinking and I know it was right, but looking at that now . . . it was meat and potatoes; it was life itself to people, opened and blew their minds. Can't do that now. I have accepted that. It was hard to accept but after a while you realize this is reality.

What difference did it make that Sinister Wisdom existed?

CN: What it did...we asked for things like fiction and poetry...also essays. We were concerned about thinking. . . it was more analyzing the kind of concepts that we had grown up with and beginning to see how they had shortchanged women. This is the feminist part of it. So what we did then, I think, was to provide a space for women who were already writers, lesbians who were already writers, and those who wanted to be. And once there was a publication, it encouraged

96 ♀ Sinister Wisdom 112- *Moon and Cormorant*

them to write about what it was to be a lesbian, what their experiences were, and to put them into fiction, essays, all of these different things. And by giving a space for people to be published, we encouraged them to write more. When I talked to Elly Bulkin, one of the editors of Conditions *in New York that started shortly after we did...what we were doing by publishing this was actually causing people to write more. Elly and her friend did an anthology of lesbian fiction and short stories. They said in their introduction that the fact that there was a place for these things to be published encouraged the development of writing. Now the first short stories that we got were interesting. Because they were primarily autobiographical and they were also quite visionary, they were science fiction kinds of things imagining a world where women lived alone, just letting the fantasies develop. Over the years the short stories became far more complex, lesbians were seen as far more complex. The first short stories had to do with coming out stories and dealing with parents, and the fear and all of that. Later they became more sophisticated. You've got to have a place to develop.*

It also, of course, developed theory. My partner was in philosophy. She was interested in analyzing what it meant to be a lesbian. And it is interesting to me that the mainstream publishers today make it look as though this has never been done before. But it has been done before.

The analysis and the theorizing in the '70s was not a game. It was very important. It was looking at something from a different standpoint. It was seeing that logic was completely male identified... from Aristotle forward is male identified. Logic is male identified, When I read Queer Theory, I think they are playing games, with words, with ideas, intellectual games. It is not something that is meaningful to you and me.

What lessons did you learn from your work on *Sinister Wisdom*?

CN: Well, for one thing, I learned how to paste up pages (ha!). I learned that you shouldn't stay in it too long. It is so political and there is so much infighting in publishing as there is in everything. We saw one press go down after another. We what I have learned now is actually, you can't change people's minds. We thought in the '70s that if women would get together, if they would bond, if they would examine what was happening to them, then we could change the world. So this was our way of doing it. Our way of doing it was not by trying to get hired in the government and try to do it that way. It was by changing people's minds. It was so sensible and...That's what all revolutionaries do. They have to go through that stage where they believe that they can change people's minds ... then you become very narrow in what you are going to tolerate in other people. We were very intolerant. What they are saying about us now is true. We were in a sense demanding something of them and they didn't get it and didn't want to. We were redefining lesbianism which made no sense to them. They say that we destroyed the whole butch femme thing and that was true. . . They said that we were not sexual but that was not true. There was a lot of sexuality in there. The role playing was wrong because that was copying the patriarchal world. If women could come together and value each other. In the patriarchy it was impossible to do that. We were very intolerant. But as you get older you move on and you look back and shudder that you could actually do that.

But it was necessary.

We were definitely political. We meant who got power? And what is power? I'm glad of that.

It was the first great commitment I ever made.

We worked part time while we were working on the magazine. After I left the university, I was able to make it financially with part time work so we were able to make it. Back then you could work part time then and make it. Reagan and the '80s changed all that. In the '70s we could work part time and that's how we were able to build a movement. In the '80s people couldn't be activists...we had to work full time then. The economy was on our side then. So all of these things changed over time.

Whom did you admire?

CN: I admired Adrienne Rich a great deal. She is a brilliant, brilliant woman and she was way ahead in her thinking. She stood up and said "I am a lesbian." She was able to come out and claim who she was and suffered from that and it was quite a lot. She is a great thinker. I admire Julia Penelope for linguistics. Also Joanna Russ and Mary Daly.

I was struck by your comments about coming out in the magazine. What was it like to come out then?

CN: It was scary. I couldn't have done it alone. I don't think I suffered for being a lesbian; I suffered for my feminism. They put it this way, "Catherine used to be such a nice person, she is so angry now." This is what feminism did to me.

SWEAT, SWEET

Minnie Bruce Pratt

East along the line of apple trees on Hawley,
the skin of the petals translucent in the sun, early,
the body and arms of the trees gleaming through.

I come closer and press my nose into the blossoms,
the fragrance of your skin, faint sweet sweat, as if
salt and all the minerals of the earth are called
up into you and alchemized by you, breathing out
through every pore what you've lived, your love,
your chemistry, your history, the smell of your skin.

LICKED

Minnie Bruce Pratt

The people we were, the people we are now.
The apple blossoms blown, flowers fallen, blight
biting into every leaf, skin scaling on the trunk
and branches, skeletal shadows on the walk
as I pass, grieving and loving this boney brittle
world that breaks and opens day after day, the bees
gnawing at the red-hearted rose-of-sharon, licked,
sticky all over, its flower tongues, pollen bristle,
until it's hard to tell the flower from the bee,
the insect from the tree, me from you, you from me.

THE TORNADO

Minnie Bruce Pratt

You and I saw the storm coming up the valley.
It made a precipice and from there it fell on us.

At the storm edge, a couplet of wind fragments
side-by-side, inbound and outbound velocities,
tried to clasp each other. Then a whirl into oblivion,
the only evidence of existence a cloud of debris.

Beauty into nothingness. You say, *Let's step back
from the window.* You clasp my hand. What will be
left of us? Bits of sound and matter, exhorting
voices inside the whirlwind saying the end is not
destruction, saying two is not the answer, saying
revolution is bigger than both of us, revolution is
a science that infers the future presence of us.

Where we still turn and turn among all other things,
among the not-yet-known we set in motion now.

TRIBUTE TO MICHELLE CLIFF

Michelle Cliff

"CREATING ALCHEMY":
ON THE WORK OF MICHELLE CLIFF

Julie R. Enszer

Michelle Cliff and Adrienne Rich edited eight issues of *Sinister Wisdom;* from 1980 through 1984, together they produced issue 17 through issue 24. Cliff and Rich were the second pair of *Sinister Wisdom* editors. They purchased the magazine from founders, Catherine Nicholson and Harriet Desmoines, and moved it to their home in Western Massachusetts. The post office box for *Sinister Wisdom* was in Amherst; Cliff and Rich lived a short distance away in Montague. The two met in New York City when Cliff was a production editor at W. W. Norton, Rich's publishing house, and had not been lovers for long when they took the reins of the journal. In her first "Notes for a Magazine," Cliff began by writing about how "lesbian/feminists must work to rededicate ourselves to a women's revolution." She continued,

> I see the need to bring up the idea of revolution because it can so easily become obscured. And as women we tend not to think in terms of revolution. The historian Blanche W. Cook has said that revolution is a process, not an event. It is a process which requires courage and vigilance. Theory and nourishment. Criticism and support. Anger. And it requires love—for ourselves— for each other. We are women and we have been taught to love: men   children. Seldom—if ever— each other. Seldom—if ever—ourselves. We have been taught—and the dominant culture continues to tell us—to direct our affection outward: not inward. To choose to love both ourselves and each other is a revolutionary choice.

In this early articulation of her intentions as editor of the journal, Cliff centers revolution with a distinctively feminist approach. Cliff articulates the necessities of theory, criticism, and anger, and reminds readers that in addition to these elements, which can be at times fractious, difficult, painful, feminists and lesbians need nourishment, support, and love. As always, reading these words from 1980, I am inspired by the palpable belief in revolution that Cliff expresses and by the method of elaborating what revolution needs in the current moment. The vision she articulates here requires balance; it must be deployed with care.

She concluded "Notes" with these words:

> I approach this editorship with a certain degree of ambivalence. I am a thirty-four-year-old woman. A lesbian. A woman of color. I have just begun to write, and I am selfish about my writing and my time. But I have made a lifetime commitment to a revolution of women. I want to serve this revolution. And I want this revolution to be for all women. I want *Sinister Wisdom* to continue to be informed by the power of women. I want to make demands on this magazine, and I want other women to make demands on it also. I want these demands to include courage and vigilance. Theory and nourishment. Criticism and support. Anger and love.

Cliff's words in this issue provide a rare view into her heavily guarded interior as her literary career was beginning. Persephone Press published Cliff's first essay collection, *Claiming an Identity They Taught Me to Despise*, in 1980 as she and Rich began editing *Sinister Wisdom*. Crossing Press published *Abeng* in 1984, as they passed the journal to the next editors Michelle Uccella and Melanie Kaye/Kantrowitz.

The editorship of Cliff and Rich and the eight issues of the journal that they produced were profoundly influential for *Sinister Wisdom*, lesbian-feminist communities, and Cliff and Rich themselves as writers. They produced *Sinister Wisdom* during a period in the Women's Liberation Movement when journals could source much of the labor for journal production from women, including printing and typesetting. Cliff and Rich printed the first three issues of *Sinister Wisdom* that they edited and published at New Victoria Printers, a woman-owned press, in Lebanon, NH. They supported Catherine Nicholson and Harriet Desmoines, the former editors and publishers of *Sinister Wisdom*, in the development of their typesetting business in Shelburne Falls, MA; Catherine and Harriet provided typesetting and paste up services for *Sinister Wisdom* 20 and *Sinister Wisdom* 21. Beginning with *Sinister Wisdom* 20, they used Iowa City Women's Press and its affiliate A Fine Bind, two women-owned companies, for support publishing the journal. The power of women that Cliff envisioned in her first "Notes for a Magazine" manifested itself as the two published the journal using women's labor and women's businesses.

Together Cliff and Rich published a raft of writers whose names became well-known in feminist and lesbian-feminist circles; often *Sinister Wisdom* was an early or first publications for (lesbian) writers. Cliff and Rich published Donna Allegra, Andrea Dworkin, Judith McDaniel, Willyce Kim, Audre Lorde, Marilyn Frye, Irena Klepfisz, Beth Brant, Judy Grahn, Paula Gunn Allen, Maureen Brady, Lee Lynch, Joanna Russ, hattie gossett, Mab Segrest, Barbara Smith, Beverly Smith, Chrystos, Susan Wood-Thompson, Gloria Anzaldúa, Barbara Deming, Judith Katz, Sarah Lucia Hoagland, wendy stevens, Selma Miriam, Valerie Minor, Joan Nestle, zana, Virginia de Araújo, Jean Sirius, Sudie Rakusin, Red Jordan Arobateau, Ann Allen Shockley, Michelle Parkerson, Jean Swallow, Minnie Bruce Pratt, Karen Brodine, Susan Sherman, Cheryl Clarke, Marilyn Hacker, Toi Derricotte, Jacqueline Lapidus, and Joy Harjo. The full series of issues and a database of contributors to issues published by Cliff and Rich as well as all other editors are available online at www.sinisterwisdom.org/archive. In addition to publishing poems, essays, interviews, short stories, reviews, art, and other creative work, Cliff and Rich curated lively

106 ♀ Sinister Wisdom 112- *Moon and Cormorant*

dialogues and debates about separatism and anti-Semitism in the pages of *Sinister Wisdom*.

Perhaps one of the most influential issues published during Cliff and Rich's editorial tenure was *Sinister Wisdom* 22/23, a special double issue edited by Beth Brant. *A Gathering of Spirit: New American Indian Women's Writing* (*Sinister Wisdom* 22/23) was a crucial articulation of Native American Indian women's writing. For at least three years after the publication of *A Gathering of Spirit*, *Sinister Wisdom* marketed and sold the issue as a Sinister Wisdom Book, ensuring that it continued to reach readers. In 1988, Firebrand Books republished it as a trade book. *A Gathering of Spirit* circulated widely and remained in print for many years, influencing generations of readers and writers. There has not been a comparable volume of Native American women's writing since.

In the introduction to the issue, Brant describes pitching the idea for an issue to Cliff and Rich during a visit on New Year's Day in 1982:

> We are sitting in their living room. Dinner is over. It has been snowing all day, the white flakes muffle any sound coming from outside. Michelle has lit the oil lamps. The light is warm yellow and soft. We are talking about writing. About women of color writing. I ask if they have ever thought of doing an issue devoted to the writing of Indian women. They are enthusiastic, ask me if I would edit such a collection. There is panic in my gut. I am not an "established" writer. (To this day, I am not sure what those words mean.) I have never edited any work but my own. And I do not have the education. And to me, that says it all. To have less than a high-school diploma is not to presume. About anything.
>
> I do not say these things out loud, only to myself. But I do say polite words--I'm sure someone else

> could do a better job, I really don't think I have the
> time, etc., etc.
>
> Michelle assures me that editing is not a mysterious
> process. It think it is. Adrienne tells me that they
> would not consider undertaking such a project. One
> is Black. One is Jewish. Neither is Indian. So I am
> caught, asking the inside me, why did I raise this if I
> wasn't willing to take it on?

This account by Brant reveals not only the texture of her mind and spirit as a writer and editor but also some of the practices of Cliff and Rich as editors. They were open to projects by other women; they demystified the process of editing both by explaining it to writers and potential editors and by creating opportunities for women to edit, and they valued and expressed the political significance of women of color editing and curating work.

Brant does take on the project of editing an issue of *Sinister Wisdom*; Cliff and Rich published *Sinister Wisdom* 22/23: *A Gathering of Spirit* in 1983. Though it seems that neither woman preserved her correspondence or notes (there is a small archive of Cliff's work at the University of Georgia; Brant's papers are not archived anywhere), I suspect that Cliff and Brant communicated regularly while Brant edited *Sinister Wisdom* 22/23. Cliff and Rich published a letter from Brant to Cliff in *Sinister Wisdom* 19 (1982). In the letter, Brant describes her experience at the Women in Print Conference in Washington DC. Dated October 6, 1981, Brant wrote the letter immediately after the conference which was held October 1-4; Brant details both her experiences at the conference and recounts some of the dynamics around race. The letter reveals affection between Brant and Cliff and also the close relationship between the two couples (Cliff and Rich and Brant and her partner Denise Dorsz); Brant writes to Cliff, "I feel so much a part of you and your life" (35), and concludes, "Dearest friend, this letter has been long, you must be tired. I look forward to seeing you soon" (36). The letter seems to gesture to an on-going correspondence documenting the strength of the friendship and the connection. During the process of creating *A Gathering of Spirit*, which Brant describes delightfully in her introduction as "a flurry of typing, going to the post office, going to the printer, making phone calls, writing more letters," I imagine Cliff offering reassurance and support to Brant for her work. I imagine the two of them with a relationship of friendship, affection, and comradeship growing through the work of *Sinister Wisdom*. In the acknowledgments, Brant thanked Cliff and Rich "for embracing my idea of an issue devoted to North American Indian women's writing and art. For helping me give it fruit. For not interfering. For friendship." These brief lines invite a larger story of friendship and political solidarity within the pages of the journal. While the documents do not exist to tell that story, readers might imagine it in the mind, in the heart.

Cliff's work in *Sinister Wisdom* was not only editorial. She published two essays in the journal and two book reviews. These four pieces lend insight into Cliff's creative work and also into the historical moment of her editorship and creative production. Editorial work demands subjectivity that is removed or abstracted from the physical and emotional intimacy of reading a text. Production editors, responsible for copyediting and proofreading as well as overseeing the design and printing of books, encounter texts as words and sentences in need of correcting, corralling, and fixing. Authors live inside a text producing it for readers to enjoy. Editors are first readers with an eye to external readers; they help an author produce a final manuscript. Production editors, the space Cliff occupied in commercial publishing, are responsible for making a book to industry standards; they discipline a text to become an object that anyone picking it up can recognize it as a book, a story, a narrative, even if what is inside it challenges these very ideas and conceptions.

Cliff's editorial work at W. W. Norton and *Sinister Wisdom* demanded this outside subjectivity, but her work as a creator challenges subjectivity. Cliff's *oeuvre* of five novels, a short story collection, and three essay collections demonstrates how colonialism and racism fracture subjectivity. Her early essays in *Sinister Wisdom* capture how these themes germinate in her writing.

"Notes on Speechlessness," published in 1978 in *Sinister Wisdom* 5, was Cliff's first essay in the journal. The piece is literally written as notes and the original publication contains a hand-drawn graphic (it is not clear if the graphic was drawn by Cliff or someone else). Reflecting on this essay in the preface to *The Land of Look Behind*, Cliff describes it as

> written in snatches on a nine-to-five job. I did not choose the note form consciously; a combination of things drew me to it. An urgency for one thing. I also felt incompetent to construct an essay in which I would describe the intimacies, fears, and lies I wrote of in "Speechlessness." I felt my thoughts, things I had held within for a lifetime, traversed so wide a terrain, had so many stops and starts, apparent non sequiturs, that an essay—with its cold-blooded dependence on logical construction, which I had mastered practically against my will— could not work. My subject could not respond to that form, which would have contradicted the idea of speechlessness. This tender approach to myself within the confines and interruptions of a forty-hour-a-week job and against a history of forced fluency was the beginning of a journey into speech. (12)

The material conditions of Cliff's life, working a nine-to-five job shaped her creative work. The broader Women's Liberation Movement and by her editorship of *Sinister Wisdom* also supported her journey into speech. Cliff's speech was strengthened and emboldened by the opportunity to publish other writers and nurture their work through *Sinister Wisdom*.

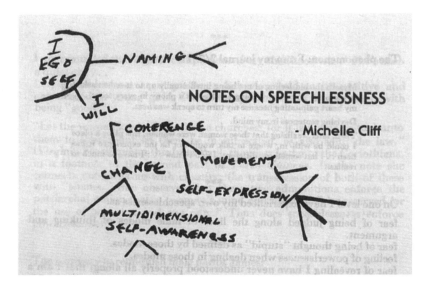

In "Notes on Speechlessness." Cliff ascribes speechless to a variety of factors, three of which she names: 1. "Being female forced into male modes of thinking and argument". 2. "Being a lesbian in the same circumstance. Concealing lesbianism and thereby entering a dual masquerade—passing straight/passing lesbian." and 3. "The symbolic origin of my speechlessness lies in an event of my childhood: the diary-reading." In this list, Cliff links speechlessness with an analysis of sex, sexual orientation, and past trauma.

In these notes, Cliff not only diagnoses the problems of women's silences, she also offers some solutions and visions for speech. In the conclusion, Cliff makes this statement for survival:

> To not be speechless: to seek those modes of thought and articulation which will assure the unity rather than the division of myself.
>
> To separate out and eliminate those elements which split me.
>
> Those elements which have divided me into mind/body, straight/lesbian, child/adult.

This means nothing more or less than seeking my own language.

This may be what women will do.

The search for a unified self is a quest that Cliff's protagonists undertake in her novels. The work of seeking her own language, work that unfolds through her writing, also emerges within the pages of *Sinister Wisdom* as Cliff curates a new language by an array of women writes reaching for unity rather than division of the self.

"Anonymity and the Denial of the Self" was the second essay by Cliff published before she and Rich became editors of the journal. "Anonymity and the Denial of the Self" was in *Sinister Wisdom* 9 published in 1979. (A selection of this essay was reprinted in the 15th anniversary issue of *Sinister Wisdom*, *Sinister Wisdom* 43/44; this issue is still available for sale from *Sinister Wisdom*). This essay, in five parts, explores another aspect of speechlessness: speech that is not owned or assigned to women but rather made anonymously. "Anonymity and the Denial of the Self" meditates first on a book about the artistic production of women painters in "an isolated district in India." The second part of the essay opens with the declaration: "The expectation of the dominant culture has always been that women will be pleasing to men; that we will efface our/selves—that we will be satisfied with, in fact long for, anonymity." Cliff then explores the meaning of anonymity on "our history (metrology) and our tradition (matriography) and our/selves (matrices)." Here Cliff comes into her power as a writer and analyst. She writes:

> When we choose to create, and to name our creations as our own, we are engaging in a radical act of separation from which, historically, we have consistently been discouraged. As women we have been taught, and have internalized the teaching, that we are extensions of others, not our/selves, and we have

112 ♀ Sinister Wisdom 112- *Moon and Cormorant*

been eager to plead for "sweet waters." By choosing anonymity we are choosing erasure. (65).

Cliff draws into this essay an array of historical sources; Felicia Hemes, Berthe Morisot, Manet, Paula Becker, Artemisia Gentileschi, Romaine Brooks, Maria van Oosterwyck, Kathe Kollwitz, and Suzanne Valadon all make an appearance as Cliff reaches to understand how "to break the constraints of role" and ultimately to expand and reimagine the role of woman.

In the early 1980s in the pages of feminist and lesbian journals, book reviewing was a vibrant political and community practice. Cliff reviewed two books for *Sinister Wisdom*. The first review, published in *Sinister Wisdom* 13 in 1980, was of Joan Gibb's collection of poetry *Between a Rock and a Hard Place*. Cliff praises Gibb's book as "heroic and powerful" as "diametrically opposed to powerlessness and to speechlessness." She says, "These are works of politics and anger. Of love and history. Of knowledge and understanding. These are the works of a black lesbian feminist woman who has refused the silences proffered her." The second review, published in *Sinister Wisdom* 19 in 1982 when Cliff edited the journal, is a review of *This Bridge Called My Back*. (This review is reprinted in *Sinister Wisdom* 43/44). Titled, "Making Soul, Creating Alchemy," the review quotes extensively from selections of *This Bridge Called My Back* and Cliff reflects on the meaning of the book to her. She describes the book as connecting "women of color across racial, sexual, class, ethnic identifications. It connects women to each other and it connects ideas to each other. But the writings in this book are always aware of the divisions forged between women of color from varying backgrounds and heritages, and the writers respect the history of these divisions while at the same time they move to mend them." Cliff's review is an early one of *This Bridge*; Cliff's passion for the book is a harbinger of its extraordinary influence.

In her final Notes for a Magazine, Rich praised Cliff as "the managing and sustaining editor, whose dedication, skill and energy kept the body and soul of *SW* together." She also noted that it "seemed truly ironic that some correspondents and contributors chose to assume that I was the "real" editor, or the only one." Cliff wrote that she learned a lot from the years of editing *Sinister Wisdom* and that it was a "good experience, although a complicated one." One of her key learnings was that "the bottom line is very powerful and that we must address the economics of this movement and how we can survive." Cliff called for more organizations, "[W]e need more institutions of our own making—more outlets for our words and thoughts, more battered women's shelters, soup kitchens for poor or unemployed women, food cooperatives, places to meet and organize." She concluded:

> We must give of our time and our money (those of us who have it is always understood) to those institutions we care about, or else this movement will become only a pastime for women who can afford it, and not something geared to make radical change in the lives of sisters everywhere.

After Cliff and Rich edited *Sinister Wisdom*, Cliff's reputation as a novelist grew. Her novels, in particular *Abeng*, *No Telephone to Heaven*, *Bodies of Water* and *Free Enterprise*, are recognized by readers as beautiful and tender; literary critics praise them similarly and situate them as important post-colonial narratives.

In 2010, I interviewed Michelle Cliff for *Lambda Literary*. The occasion was the release of her new novel, *Into the Interior*. The book, Cliff's final novel, is challenging; it is an evocative book that relies on pastiche more than narrative. The language is lush yet sparse; the ideas and emotions seem compelling, but it is a difficult book to enter, write about, and understand. My interview with Cliff was challenging as well. I had just begun editing *Sinister Wisdom*; and I imagined a kinship with her because she had edited the journal. Though of course to say that she had edited the journal is to inadvertently diminish her work. Cliff was a key administrator of the journal at a time when it was booming and had an extraordinary reach. To say *Sinister Wisdom* is to name a journal that a small community of readers know and love; to say, *Sinister Wisdom*, edited during the early 1980s by Adrienne Rich and Michelle Cliff, is to situate the journal in a pantheon. In preparing to interview Cliff, I realized that what I wanted from Cliff was sisterhood; to state it even more plainly: I wanted to bond with her. What I received were curt email replies. I was solicitous and, I thought, engaging; Cliff felt cool over the few emails we exchanged. In my raft of questions, more questions were left unanswered than answered. Her replies were brief, some even terse. I struggled to produce a piece that highlighted her work, her new book. I was younger then, a star-struck writer who perhaps did not give Cliff all her due. All I know is I wanted something from that interaction that I did not receive. It haunts me. I only write this because Cliff wrote in "Anonymity and the Denial of the Self": "To admit the personal counts is a radical act for a woman (68)." This is my admission of the personal. Our brief email exchanges from 2010, the interview we constructed together, remain, nearly a decade later, uncomfortable (and unsatisfying) encounter. It haunts me. Then I read Cliff's novels; read her contributions to *Sinister Wisdom*. Imagine her labor to make this journal possible. They inspire me. They remind me of my commitments. In "Anonymity," Cliff also writes, "To be a feminist is to attempt the rescue of other women from the various constraints which culminate in anonymity" (70). This dossier is an attempt to rescue Cliff from various constraints.

Michelle Cliff died on June 12, 2016, the same day as the massacre at the Pulse nightclub in Orlando, FL. This tribute to Cliff is fittingly a part of an issue that lifts up political writing by lesbians. Both the work of publishing political writing by lesbians and recognizing the life and work of Michelle Cliff are crucial to *Sinister Wisdom*. In this dossier on Cliff, you will find contemporary writers responding to the work of Cliff, photographs courtesy of Michelle Cliff's estate, a complete bibliography of her work, and a reprint of her powerful essay on speechlessness.

I offer these words as a tribute to Cliff, in the pages of a journal that continues to publish in part thanks to Cliff's labors many years ago, and I also implore all of the readers of this work, readers who are our subscribers today and readers in the future who might be reading this words in a library, in some new format online or in some type of replica of a book that I cannot yet even imagine, to read more of Cliff's work and engage with it in a meaningful and powerful way. Novels, essays, stories, book reviews. Cliff left an impressive corpus of work that challenges us to think about the world in new ways. This dossier extends an invitation to engage Cliff, to rescue her today and many days in the future "from the various constraints which culminate in anonymity." Each time Michelle Cliff's name appears on the inside cover of an issue of *Sinister Wisdom*, it is a feminist act to challenge anonymity. Take the feminist act of reading Cliff's work. Each time a reader picks up her books, reads her work, it is a feminist act challenging anonymity and speechlessness.

Joan Nestle and Michelle Cliff

Michelle Cliff and Adrienne Rich with a book

FINDING MICHELLE CLIFF

Yasmin Tambiah

Summer, 1986. I was in New York City for my first Lesbian and Gay Pride March. I had come in from a university on Long Island, where I was working on a Master's degree, and was staying with my friend Utsa in Brooklyn. Utsa was co-editor of "Anamika," the first ever South Asian lesbian newsletter, and was also in graduate school. We had been introduced by a mutual friend, and often met up to share stories about being South Asian, South Asian and lesbian, and South Asian lesbians living in the USA. There were extremely few other South Asian lesbians we knew of at the time; we were a special community to each other, even though we had circles of American friends and feminist comrades, both women of color and white. We looked out for works by women of color, especially lesbian, and read whatever we found – Native American and Latina, African American and Asian American.

But something was missing in the messages from these writings. While they were powerful, moving, inspiring and thought-provoking, they all were framed by, and almost exclusively referenced, the United States of America. That evening before the March, in between watching the TV broadcast of the documentary, *The Times of Harvey Milk*; discussing whether we should in some way disguise ourselves before we marched (we were on student visas, and concerned we might be deported for being queer); and talking about *This Bridge Called My Back: Writings by Radical Women of Color,* I told Utsa that I couldn't relate fully to what I read or to the political priorities of our American sisters of color. She agreed. She was from India, I from Sri Lanka. Our feminisms were derived from nationalist struggles against British colonialism, and postcolonial complications; mediating interethnic, interreligious and class hostilities; and engaging in the South Asian and international women's movements. Our lesbian identities too were forged in that crucible, profoundly challenging as this was.

118 ♀ Sinister Wisdom 112- *Moon and Cormorant*

Then Utsa said, "You should read Michelle Cliff. She speaks to us."

That weekend in New York City I bought *Claiming an Identity They Taught Me to Despise.* From the first words of "Passing" to the last of "Separations," I read, and re-read. Many times. Everything was familiar — even when details sometimes weren't. The Caribbean and South Asia. Parallel experiences and different specifics. Crisscrossings of oceans and continents. Subtleties of coloring. Being "out" and "in" because of how a body was read. Class classifications, colored class and classed genders. Women's mandatory labors — at home, plantations, factories. The old and the new, what was and what could be, points of departure and jetties for returns, all offered from an internationalist perspective to which I could relate. This included issues particular to the USA, and approaches that connected America with other histories and geographies.

Michelle Cliff spoke to me, then and over the subsequent years as few others have done, across many different lands and seas. Wherever I've lived I've collected her writings, her art of telling in-depth, broad-canvas stories in precise, spare language a model I try to follow in my own work.

Claiming an Identity They Taught Me to Despise still keeps me company, still speaks to me 30 years on as I write this, based in Sydney, Australia.

I miss Michelle deeply.

(MICRO) AGGRESSIONS

Ashley-Luisa Santangelo

"Speechlessness--as I have known it to be--is implosive, not explosive. That is, it is most effective against
the speechless person."
- Michelle Cliff

At the time I read Michelle Cliff's *Notes on Speechlessness*, I thought that the really rough years of my personal anger were over. I thought that I had mellowed out, grew a thick skin, and learned how to take care of myself. However, reading *Notes on Speechlessness*, caused all my anger to come roaring back.

Everyone believes that they can spot a racist, a sexist, a misogynist; put them in their place, fight back, win. However, what many don't realize is that they are talking about salient, in-your-face attacks on a person. Microaggressions are just the opposite. They are small, cold, and sharp as a needle. Getting stuck with one needle hurts but sometimes, it can be shrugged off. Getting stuck with ten, twenty, fifty needles a day and you'll end up drawing blood.

Microaggressions are painful because they are disrespectful and harsh displays of power. They are most painful because they are the most silent attack and are hardest to combat. With it comes a wave of helplessness. How do you prove your value as a complex person who breathes and feels and experiences the world? People in power use microaggressions to take power away from others they perceive as less than. Their victims turn into bodies, into numbers. It strips away dignity. It dismisses the victim as nothing.

Often microaggressions are brushed off by abusers. "It didn't mean anything" or "It was just a joke". Just a joke? Really? Who's laughing? That is often the excuse. If it is, it is only the one in power who has the privilege to laugh. But what about when someone

120 ♀ Sinister Wisdom 112- *Moon and Cormorant*

you trust uses a microaggression to explain to you the differences between you? As in my story, people we begin to trust or love can make us feel inferior and other by assuming that the divides between us are insurmountable barriers. First, this demeans and discredits where we come from as women, as queer, as PoC. Second, it disvalues our ability to change, to bridge barriers, to grow together, and to develop as human beings.

Cliff's *Notes on Speechlessness* calls attention to the internal harm that victims of microaggressions suffer. Implosion. The pain of exploding from the inside. A seemingly contained, personal shattering. I spent many years trying to prove myself as a woman, as a Colombian-American, as a first generation, as a cycle-breaker, the list goes on. At first, I exiled myself from what made me who I am. Then I exiled others from myself as I began to accept myself for who I am. It wasn't until I found a supportive PoC community that I began heal. It wasn't I began to understand who I was in my roots, that I began to grow.

***

9:48 AM Thursday, June 28th

The refrigerator door released a suction noise as it gave way to her pull. Hooking her fingers in the handle of the milk container, Jude ignored the stale smell coming from one of the many crumbled clusters of bagged lunches and returned to her coffee mug next to the machine. After fixing her coffee, she settled in on the terrace table with her notepad and journal. Paul arrived shortly after, as was the morning routine that they became accustomed to after two years of working together. Halfway through her coffee, Paul would come in, his shoes clipping on the tiled floor. He would have a pastry bag in one hand, blue paper cup in the other, polite-business-appropriate smile on his face.

" 'morning!"

"G'dmorning", Jude's pen scritch-scratched as the ball rolled ink in swift curves across the lined paper. She did not look up.

Spring 2019 ♀ 121

Inevitably, Paul would begin once he unwrapped the croissant from its pastry sheet. Pausing over his unwrapped goods, he sighed.

"What." Jude was still writing. Flipping to the printed calendar she taped to the cover, checking the dates and times for meetings, drawing little squares on her to do list to check off later; this habitual organization of her life helped her feel some semblance of control.

"I realize I need to save more money."

"You realize you need to save more money."

"Okay, I know I need to save more money. I just need to think of ways to do it."

"Start bringing your lunches from home." Jude paused and looked at him. Even though she suggested it, she struggled to imagine Paul adding to the plastic bag hodge-podge in the fridge, containers labeled with his name, washing dishes in the communal sink.

"Yeah..."

By his lack of enthusiasm, she knew he couldn't imagine it either. He took a bite of his pastry, politely licked crumbs off his lips and looked up towards the sun. Jude returned to double checking her list. When she finished, she sat back in her chair and let her arms go limp on the armrests. She could almost feel the sun being absorbed by her melanin and smiled at the return of the early-summer sun. She imagined for the millionth time what it might be like to live with her family in New Mexico again, with its dry heat and miles of wide-open space.

"I got an idea." Paul brightened at the thought.

"What?" Jude kept her face up towards the sun, her body full of warmth.

"You could make my lunches and I could pay you. How about five dollars a piece?"

Jude blinked, then sat up abruptly.

"What are you asking me?" She could have laughed. She was dumbfounded.

"What? Seems fair to me. You bring your lunches, just make a little extra for me. Besides, you're part time, you could use the money right? Isn't that what women are good at?"

Jude closed her eyes. Deep breaths, girl. Today is not the day to lose it. Today is not the day to lose your job. Keep it together. She thought of her mother, pretended she was there coaching her through this moment. She bit her bottom lip and took that deep breath.

"Ahh, No. Definitely no."

She gathered her books, her pen, and her mug. She could hear nothing but the rushing of her blood in her own ears. Too frustrated to wait for the elevator, Jude raced down the back stairs, her grip so tight her nails left half moon imprints along the spine of her notebook.

1:23 PM

The elevator arrived at the 6th floor and paused two minutes before its heavy metallic door screeched open. Jude braced herself before pushing the heavy second door open. Here was another lunch spent tolerating the cow-chewers aka the individuals who made it to middle-age never learning how to chew with their mouth closed. However, her relief was almost palpable when she saw Magdalena sitting alone at the end of the terrace table. Maybe everyone decided to go out for lunch today?

"Maggie, you have no idea how relieved I am to see you right now", Jude said, falling into an open seat in the sun.

"Damn, did you have a rough morning too?"

"You don't even want to know. It will just make your blood boil." Jude said, beginning to unbag her lunch. They both relaxed in each other's company and settled deeper into their seats. A warm, thick breeze blew, whipping up their hair. They both inhaled to their lungs' full capacity, trying to take as much in as possible before exhaling.

The open terrace door, warped from years of rain exposure, closed with a shuttered bang, startling them, and causing them to both look at the door. Jude felt her whole body tense as she looked up to see Bethany stomping over to join them. Maggie looked at her. Here we go again, they expressed silently to each other.

"Aaaww, look at how cute you both are with your little lunch boxes!" Bethany said, sitting down across from them. Maggie blinked one long blink in Jude's direction before turning towards her phone. "Hi, Beth," she said without commitment.

"So you guys, what are we going to do this weekend?" said Beth with mock enthusiasm, flicking her gaze between the two of them. Neither of them were keen on answering. "Oh, I know, we can go to this bar near my place that has these giant nacho platters" she rushed on like an unavoidable freight train on a one-way track, "and we can rip Maggie's weight watchers card from her so she can enjoy herself for a change. You'd probably benefit from a plate too, Jude, since you're all skin and bones."

Unnoticed by Bethany, Jude and Maggie instinctively sucked their teeth. Jude could feel the heat coming from Maggie's direction, and knew she was pissed. She knew that Maggie had spent the better part of the year working on her relationship with food so that she could live freer, uninhibited by fear or pressure or self-hate. Unlike herself, who was struggling daily with her image in the mirror. Why did it seem like her body was always shifting in the mirror? Why did her wrists seem so skinny? So easily breakable? After her grandfather's funeral, she covered the mirrors so that his soul wouldn't get trapped in that interdimensional limbo of polished glass and metal. Already three months later and she hadn't removed the covers; yet that fragile version of herself seemed to live there, behind the curtain of sheets, quietly awaiting further inspection. Looking down at her plate, her leftovers from the night before, once desirable now seemed revolting. Jude fought the repulsion rising up in her and took another bite.

As Jude chewed, Maggie retorted, "No, we're busy with recording new music this weekend. But next time you want company, best not to insult the people you're inviting out."

Bethany flapped her hand to dismiss Maggie's response, nervous smile pinching her face. "Oh come on, I was just kidding!" Her voice came out like a high pitched whine. "Maggie, you can be so uptight! You know I was kidding, right Jude?"

Jude swallowed a second repulsive bite of food. Looking into Bethany's eyes she could see the fear, and also, the self-loathing. How many times had people walked away from her, stopped engaging with her, because of her mouth? Because in all her years no one ever taught her how to speak without insulting? Holding her gaze, Jude replied, "Kidding or not, you don't have a right to make comments on other people's bodies; especially not mine."

Bethany rolled her eyes and let out an indignant sigh. "Alright, I'm sorry okay? Geez," she replied, before taking a bite of burrito and chewing it with her mouth open.

Maggie looked at Jude, who looked back at Maggie. A breeze blew strands of Maggie's hair across her face, getting caught on her eyelashes. Jude looked back at her food and felt she had no appetite. Unable to finish eating and frustrated, she packed up the remainder of her lunch and took it inside to stuff back in the community fridge. Maybe she would eat it tomorrow, but she couldn't be sure.

6:17PM

The train rumbled into a slow halt. Stuck on the D train on the Manhattan Bridge. Again. Jude looked over towards the lower waterfront of Manhattan. The water was rolling peacefully, lapping at the shores and the sides of the boats that sailed by. She felt her phone vibrate in her purse. Who was it now?

Oh, Jane. A flood of warm feeling moved through Jude as she remembered the flash of her smile, the feeling of soft skin, and the smell of the rain caught in Jane's hair the last time she had seen her.

Jude read the text message and then let out a frustrated puff of air. She read it over a second time.

> Hey Jude, I wanted to talk with you. I had a great time with you the other night, but I think we should just support each other as friends. There seems to be a lot of differences between us, little things like our schedules but also big things like our cultures and our career paths. I'm sorry if you feel I have mislead you. I didn't mean for that to happen. Best of luck, and well, see you around.

Another small sigh. Then Jude typed out a short reply.

> No love lost. Best of luck in your future endeavors. Please return my copy of Caveworld at your earliest convenience.

Short and bitter. Well, wasn't that enough? What was she even referring to when she said "differences in our cultures"? *That has to be the stupidest ending to anything I've been through* Jude, thought as leaned her head on her arm. *Maybe if I had been French or Dutch or hell, even Swedish, there wouldn't have been a problem with our "cultural differences".* Jude tried to relax but couldn't help thinking how selfish that one remark was. The D train began its slow descent into the Brooklyn underground. Five more stops and she would be home.

Home. The safe impenetrable shelter from the rest of the world. Jude sat at the kitchen table, a glass of sangria in front of her, heels lying haphazard on the floor where she dropped them. Already, the fading sunlight was blocked by the neighboring apartment building and the room took on a dull twilight glow. The cat slept on the window sill next to her chair, and she petted its small fuzzy ears. In the semi-darkness, the sangria beginning to take hold, Jude felt her muscles begin to relax from the tension of the day. She released an involuntary sigh and the physical relief sent a cool tingling sensation down her spine.

Alone and secure, she felt her appetite returning. The cat jumped down from the windowsill and followed her into the kitchenette. Soon her senses were awakened as chopped vegetables sizzled. The rich odor of garlic, the stinging smell of onions, she bit into the soft firm cap of a mushroom and thought of its soft scented musk. The cat looked up at her expectantly as she pressed the heel of her palm into a slice of plantain, flattening it before sliding it into a frying pan of oil.

Dirty pots and pans soaked in sudsy water while Jude finished off her plate. She took another sip of sangria and let its citrus taste cut across the oil and salt on her tongue. She was full. *Safe at home,* she thought, as tears began to fall from beneath her glasses.

CLIFF NOTES:
ON IDENTITY, MEMORY, AND COMMUNITY

Red Washburn

I am remembering how I learned history. Memorize this fact. Know this date. Know this president. Know this war. Know this map. Know this concept. Know this tactic. Know this rhetoric. Know all these boring details, but do not know structural power. Michelle Cliff writes, "How do we capture the history that remains only to be imagined?" This question begs us to inquire about knowledge and power as connected to "fictive history."

What is history? I remember in sixth grade the teacher, my misogynistic father with his wicked mustache out, spoke about the founding fathers. He read off of antiquated notes, yellowed like his smoke-reeking fingers. He insisted they left England on a quest for life, liberty, and the pursuit of happiness. They won the American Revolution, fighting for and establishing a new nation that promoted democracy and equality. They penned the Constitution, to which citizens were accountable. There was justice for all.

Whose history? I remember in college the professor spoke about the fathers differently, as unfounders. She pounded the podium with her fist, reverberating off chalkboards like chants in bullhorns. She offered a historical corrective: they left England because they did not want to pay British taxes, stole land from Native Americans, enslaved them and Black people, raped women, slaughtered children, and pillaged those communities with their smallpox blankets. They wrote their treaties to preserve their wealth and power. There was no justice for all.

---

128 ♀ Sinister Wisdom 112- *Moon and Cormorant*

What is struggle? I remember in grad school the professor spoke about history as a site of resistance. She asked us to pop a hole in a piece of paper, look through it, and see another angle of vision. She showed us how small actions matter in numbers. Marginalized people revolted, wanting the right to be free, to exist, to live, to be. They took to the streets, advocating for civil rights, women's rights, indigenous rights, LGBTQ rights, among others. They marched on Washington, defended themselves at Stonewall, protected Pine Ridge, protested the Miss America Pageant, and organized sits in at Woolworth's, among others. They got the right to vote, to have abortions, to get divorced, to work, to get housing, to get food, to not be harassed. They wanted freedom and liberation for all.

Whose voice? I remember all the subversive women, gender nonconforming, genderqueer, non-binary, and trans folks, and queer writers, artists, historians, and theorists I have gotten my hands on for various feminist knowledge projects the last fifteen years as a scholar, writer, and professor. Shout out to Virginia Woolf, Assata Shakur, Emma Donoghue, Gloria Anzaldúa, Monique Wittig, Cherrie Moraga, Mary Dorcey, Ailbhe Smyth, June Jordan, Judith Butler, Jack Halberstam, Leslie Feinberg, Marsha P. Johnson, Sylvia Rivera, Joan Nestle, and Michelle Cliff, among many others. I read their stories, their testimonies, and their voices, as well as assigned them to my students. The way people remember their ancestors and represent themselves is a form of cultural citizenship and radical truth-telling in a world that expects silence as compliance.

I am challenging how I learned history. I have learned from many radical thinkers how to evaluate knowledge through the spectrum of difference and power. As Elsa Barkley Brown says,

"History is everybody talking at once, multiple rhythms being played simultaneously. The events and people we write about did not occur in isolation but in dialogue with a myriad of other people and events. [. . .] As historians we try to isolate one conversation and to explore it, but the trick is then how to put that conversation in a context which makes evident its dialogue with so many others." As Joan Nestle states, "To live without history is like to live like an infant, constantly amazed and challenged by a strange and unnamed world. There is a deep wonder in this kind of existence, a vitality of curiosity and a sense of adventure that we do well to keep alive all of our lives. [. . .] To live with history is to have a memory not just of our lives but the lives of others, people we have never met but whose voices and actions connect to our collective selves. [. . .] Because of the work of grassroots national and international lesbian and gay historians, we have found patterns both in our oppression and in our responses. We can begin to analyze what went wrong and what went right. [. . .] History makes us, at one and the same time, part of a community and alone as we watch the changes come. [. . .] Living with history may be burdensome, but the alternative is exile. We would never have the chance to embrace each other, to urge each other on and telling the whole story. [. . .] The choices we make based on these voices and our own lives is the living gift we bequeath to our lesbian daughters. Every present becomes the past, but caring enough to listen will keep us all alive." Angela Davis remarks, "We are thankful for the legacies, but we do not receive them uncritically." Taken together, I hear the echoes of these women's and trans voices as I create my own critical voice. I have been thinking about the dialogues we have across time and space, those with and between intergenerational dykes, queers, gender nonconforming, non-binary, genderqueer, and trans folks in diverse communities, both as unliving and living herstory and theirstory. Herstory and theirstory are nonlinear, memory is asymmetrical, and testimony is an ongoing feminist

130 ♀ Sinister Wisdom 112- *Moon and Cormorant*

trans project, but how do we create a world that bridges then and now and where we are traveling on our own without a colonial and white supremacist map?

I am learning my herstory and theirstory. As Michelle Cliff writes, "I am untangling the filaments of my history." I remember reading and taking notes on Cliff in grad school, first in Contemporary Women's Autobiography, second in Postcolonial Literature and Theory, third in Caribbean Literature, fourth in my own undergrad class Sexuality and Literature, and lastly in Lez Create: Dyke Arts Workshop June 2016, just after her death, the day of the Pulse shootings. We sat around the table at the Lesbian Herstory Archives with its numerous queer feminist spirits. We propped our heads up, pushed up our ears, flipped pages in books, and stared at signs that read "sisterhood feels good, and saw a painting of two women's nipples touching, as we read our ancestors who have passed on recently --Audre Lorde, Adrienne Rich, Leslie Feinberg, Jeanne Cordova, and Michelle Cliff, among others. "This is their headquarters; where they write history. Around tables they exchange facts–details of the unwritten past. Like the women who came before them–the women they are restoring to their work/ space–the historians are skilled at unraveling lies; are adept at detecting the reality beneath the erasure," Michelle Cliff writes in "Against Granite." We pulled *Claiming an Identity They Taught Me to Despise* off the shelf, read "Passing," exchanged feedback on systems of discrimination—racism, sexism, classism, heterosexism, and colonialism—listened to her read "Notes on Speechlessness," and used a writing prompt on gender, power, and difference. We read her back alive and gave ourselves permission to be. We listen to her words in our own voices. We hear her legacy and speak back to her with authority. We have our own identity and authenticity, but she is part of our ancestry and community.

She was one of our trailblazers, but we are the shapeshifters now. "The historians—like those who came before them—mean to survive," Cliff still whispers to her sisters and other siblings through her writing.

What is herstory now? I remember Nancy Bereano's Firebrand and Phase 1's *The L Word* screenings and annual Phasefests. I even remember Ginger's as dyke and trans-friendly exclusive, before cis and straight people and cis and gay men co-opted it. I even remember Bluestockings when it carried *Sinister Wisdom*, before the entire journal was written off as transphobic, including me as an out genderqueer, nonbinary, trans, and gender non-conforming contributor to it, by the same circles who label the entire second-wave as transphobic. I even remember Women's, Gender, and Sexuality Studies programs and dyke marches when there were no cis straight or gay men in them. I remember the Michigan Womyn's Music Festival from the butch struts to the trans allies in understanding workshops – the hopes and the blocks. I remember archiving it. I remember editing a book about it. I still remember my writing about it. I remember the feeling of being there. I still find places and spaces where lesbian/ queer feminist culture is honored – Sisterspace, People Called Women, the Lesbian Herstory Archives, Otherwild, the NYC Dyke March, Henrietta Hudson, the Hobart Women Writers Festival, Women in Bloom, Million Women Drummers, *Sinister Wisdom*, and Women's and Gender Studies conferences, programs, and events, among others. However, power and privilege, coupled with rampant misogyny and ageism, have created the erasure of many lesbian feminist separatist spaces. I worry deeply about the survival of the remaining ones in queer, gay, and trans communities, and I also worry deeply about egregious transmisogyny and transphobia in some lesbian feminist spaces. I worry about the consequences of struggle without solidarity – the alternative to

132 ♀ Sinister Wisdom 112- *Moon and Cormorant*

our alternatives – that maintain the hegemonic power structure within which marginalized communities are trying to live and trying to survive.

What is the future of herstory, theirstory, and other stories? I neither want to think about lesbian herstory as a mere past, nor queer and trans futures just as a contentious and/or inaccurate archive. I want to honor the unliving herstory, to engage with both living herstory and theirstory, and to create intergenerational spaces in which feminism, anti-racism, and anti-colonialism are centered and pluralized. I want to preserve and celebrate our collective inheritance and refine and re-create the present and the future by designing and promoting autonomous zones that center lesbian/ queer feminist experiences and realities, but also are safe and welcoming to people who exist outside of gender and sexual binaries – trans folks across the spectrum, FTMs, MTFs, agenders, bigenders, genderfucking folks, gender outlaws, genderqueers, nonbinary folks, and other gender-nonconforming folks, etc. – and these spaces not to be dominated by white folks. I toggle in between these spaces as someone who straddles both the political category of andro, butch, masc, and dyke, and also personal identities of queer, genderqueer, nonbinary, and trans – the personal is still political. I do not want to live in a world where someone cannot respect the language or leadership of women anymore than someone who cannot respect the language or solidarity of someone outside the binary system. They are both feminist issues within lesbian and queer spaces, and we are losing them due to horizontal hostility in ways gay men and trans people are getting more access and visibility. I want a world that transforms the possibilities between lesbian and queer spaces for women and trans folks across the spectrum.

I imagine a world where the "'L' does not disappear," as Bonnie Morris puts it. A world where the "Q" does not dominate in ways "G" still does. Where "women" is not removed from Women's and Gender Studies. Where "T" represents more than FTM and MTF and the spectrum of gender and difference. Where "lesbian" is not footnoted in Queer Studies. I imagine a world where our language and communities share, work, and grow together in solidarity yet can build solidarities across difference with old, new, and emerging words and identities in time. I imagine cultures of resistance of history then, herstory, then and now, theirstory, here and now, herstories, theirstories, and other possible stories then and there.

CLAIMING AN IDENTITY
THEY TAUGHT ME TO DESPISE

Michelle Cliff

"**W**as anyone in this class not born in the United States?" the teacher asked us in the fifties. I was in third grade. I stood up and mumbled, "Jamaica," and became the focus of their scrutiny. I filled their silence with rapid lies.

Still in the third grade, I kept after school for talking. My mother—young and thin, a pale gray coat which falls from squared-off shoulders, her brown hair long and turned under at her neck—comes to fetch me. As she confronts the teacher I begin to cry, my guilt and shame at bringing her into this strange place overcomes me.

I want to protect her from their scrutiny and what they will never understand.

I.

Bertha! Bertha! The wind caught my hair and it streamed outward like wings. It might bear me up, I thought, if I jumped to those hard stones.

--Jean Rhys, *Wide Sargasso Sea*

Grace Poole gave him a cord, and he pinioned [her arms] behind her: with more rope, which was at hand, he bound her to a chair.

--Charlotte Bronte, *Jane Eyre*

pinion: the distal part of a bird's wing, including the carpus, the metacarpus, the phalanges; a wing—as a noun.

pinion: to cut off the pinion of a wing to prevent flight; to disable or restrain by binding the wings or arms, especially close to the body; to bind the wings or arms of; to shackle; to confine— *as a verb.*

To imagine I am the sister of Bertha Rochester. We are the remainders of slavery—residue:

white cockroaches
white niggers
quadroons
octoroons
mulattos
creoles
white niggers.

Her hair became wings with the interference of the wind. And she smashed *on those hard stones*. Did the sockets pain her as *he bound her to a chair* with his swift and assured grasp? And Grace Poole, the alcoholic female keeper: what were her thoughts?

Pressed into service, moved into the great house—early on.
Daughters of the masters/whores of the masters
At one with the great house/
    at odds with the great house
Setting fire to the great house/ the masters/
    sometimes ourselves.

Early on I worried about children. Tales of throwback were common. Tell-tale hair, thick noses and heavy mouths—you could be given away so easily. Better remain unbred.

II.

Creole: (the Fr. Form of *criollo,* a West Indian, probably a negro corruption of the Span. *criadillo,* the dim. of *criado,* one bred or reared, from *criar,* to breed, a derivative of the Lat. *creare,* to create.) ... It is now used of the descendants of non-aboriginal races born and settled in the West Indies, in various parts of the American mainland, and in Mauritius, Réunion, and some other places colonized by Spain, Portugal, France, or ... by England .... The use of the word by some writers as necessarily implying a person of mixed blood is totally erroneous; in itself "creole" has

136 ♀ Sinister Wisdom 112- *Moon and Cormorant*

no distinction of colour; a creole may be a person of European, negro, or mixed extraction – or even a horse .... The difference in type between the creoles and European races from which they have sprung, a difference often considerable, is due principally to changed environment – especially to the tropical or semi-tropical climate of the lands they inhabit.

-- *Encyclopedia Britannica*, 11th edition

They can always fall back on the landscape—the sudden storms—the sun which burns even as it warms. The *changed environment* of red dirt, volcanic sand, sea-eggs whose spikes wash out with piss. Alligators. Jellyfish. Oysters who cling to pilings, to be sliced off with the sharp stroke of the *machete*. The high grass of sugar cane etching fine lines into bare legs. The extravagant blossoms which release strange aromas into the too-warm air. The bright moonlight spun with these perfumes. These are their clichés—a thin film covering the real.

To imagine I am the sister of Annie Palmer
"white witch"
creole bitch
imported to the north coast of Jamaica—
legend of the island
mistress of Rose Hall
guilty of husband-murder three times over.

We drove past Rose Hall often when I was a child. They repeated her life to me. They indicated the three coconut trees she used for grave-markers. They told me she practiced *obeah* and drank the white-men's blood for power and slept with the black overseer who killed her for infidelity.

And a rich Jamaican family brought the staircase where she died and instructed their servants not to wash the blood off.

My blood commenced early. The farther back you go the thicker it becomes. And the mother is named the link, the carrier—the source of the Nile. Did she attend each birth with caution? Waiting to see the degree of our betrayal?

"Pork!" the streetcleaner called.
Pigskin scraped clean.
"You not us. You not them either."

III.

I find a broadside from nineteenth-century America.
The statement: *a creole may be . . . even a horse* is illuminated.
RAFFLE
Mr. Joseph Jennings respectfully informs his friends and the public that, at the request of many acquaintances, he has been induced to purchase from Mr. Osborne of Missouri, the celebrated Dark Bay Horse, "Star," aged five years, square trotter and warranted sound: with a new light Trotting Buggy and Harness. Also the dark, stout Mulatto Girl, "Sarah," aged about twenty years, general house servant, valued at *nine hundred dollars*, and guaranteed, and will be raffled for at 4 o'clock p.m., February first, at the selection hotel of the subscribers. The above is as represented and those persons who may wish to engage in the usual practice of raffling, will, I assure them, be perfectly satisfied with their destiny in this affair.

They name us. They buy us and sell us.

I am twenty-two and sitting in my mother's kitchen. She is about to inform me "officially." I question her delay. "I didn't think it mattered"—as if to say, "I didn't think you'd mind." "You don't know what it was like when we first came here. No one wanted to be colored. Your father's family was always tracing me. And these Americans, they just don't understand. My cousin was fired from her job in a department store when they found out she was passing. I stopped seeing her because your father was always teasing me about my colored cousin. Things are different now. You're lucky you look the way you do, you could get any man. Anyone says anything to you, tell them your father's white."

IV.

I wish to stay here in the dark ... where I belong.
--*Wide Sargasso Sea*

I dreamed there was a record album called *Black Women.* The front of the album was a baroque painting depicting a galleon on rough seas—sailing over a dragon which was visible on either side of the bow. Inset was the portrait of a large light-skinned woman—in a white turban and plain white bodice: dressed as a slave. This woman was also at the helm of the galleon and was identified in fine writing as the first black navigator. The painting, the writing continued, had been taken from a manuscript entitled *Emergam,* Munich, 1663. The dream continued—I interviewed two white women historians who told me the manuscript had been proved a fake. We argued about the false and the real but they were adamant.

(*Emergam* is the first-person future of the Latin verb *emergere:* to rise up, emerge, free oneself.)

V.

These pictures were in watercolours. The first represented clouds low and livid, rolling over a swollen sea: all the distance was in eclipse; so too was the foreground; or, rather, the nearest billows, for there was no land. One gleam of light lifted into relief a half-submerged mast, on which sat a cormorant, dark and large, with wings flecked with foam; its beak held a gold bracelet, set with gems ... a drowned corpse glanced through the green water; a fair arm was the only limb clearly visible, whence the bracelet had been washed or torn.
--*Jane Eyre*

This is the vision of Jane Eyre, small and pale. She is speaking of us. We dwell in the penumbra of the eclipse. In the half-darkness. They tell us the dark and light lie beyond us. "I feel sorry for you," the dark woman said, "You don't know who you are."

The ship in the vision has foundered. The cormorant has taken her place and surveys the damage. Her dark plumage is wet, so we know who has taken the bracelet from the white woman's arm. *The large dark bird sits with wings pinioned in the wooden chair.*

It would seem the cormorant has replaced the dragon in my dream: but no, she is the navigator, expressed by another, stripped of her power. She nests on high and dives deep into warm waters. She has green eyes and is long-lived. (It came down to this: my eyes might save me. Green-blue. Almost blue. Changing with each costume.)

VI.

I have seen the wreckage of sugar mills covered with damp and green mosses. When the concrete cracks across, green veins trace the damage. There are tracks where mules used to circle— to crush the cane. There are copper cauldrons once used to boil the juice, from which molasses and foam were drawn off to make rum. (The purest rum—do I have to say it?—is colorless and called white. Other rum is colored artificially, taking on the darkness of the casks over time—they think the golden tint makes it more appealing. The final type is colored by impurities and was once called Negro rum.)

There are great houses throughout this island abandoned to the forest.

A great aunt keeps a chipped crystal doorknob—a solid polyhedron—on the dining table of her pensioner's flat in England: "From our place at Dry Harbour," she explains. "Fancy...every door had one."

etness spreads through the wooden house. Damp spots emerge through French wallpaper where children spin thin hoops along gravel walkways. And women glide with frilled umbrellas. This is not part of us: this nineteenth-century scene of well-being. Better to look in the shacks built in the back, where newsprint covered the walls. And calendars advertised the English royal family.

VII.

The white-haired woman sits with rice piled on her dinner plate. I am ten years old and we are visiting a branch of the family. She is my first encounter with the island I left when I was three. She is the first encounter I remember. "More rice!" she screams at the woman who serves the table. And rice is brought. "More rice!" again. My sister—who is six—and I giggle. There is a woman at the head of the table who screams for rice. The mound is high. The grains slide down the mound and onto the white cloth. "No more rice," she closes.

VIII.

You are trying to make me into someone else, calling me by another name. I know, that's *obeah* too.
--*Wide Sargasso Sea*
The Alms House at May Pen is yellowing wood. It stands above a long flight of wooden steps with a narrow handrail. There is— whenever we pass—a crowd at the top of the stairs, gathered in the yard of the Alms House. I always ask about these people. Somewhere I have confused them with lepers. "Are they lepers?" I ask my father. "No, not lepers; just people with no place to go."

ACKNOWLEDGEMENT:

"Claiming an Identity They Taught Me to Despise" by Michelle Cliff originally appeared in the book by the same title. Used with permission of the Estate of Michelle Cliff.

Michelle Cliff and Adrienne Rich

SNAPSHOT CELEBRATION OF LESBIAN LOVE

Renate Klein & Susan Hawthorne begin this new segment, curated by Roberta Arnold, sharing their love for each other with the *Sinister Wisdom* community. What may seem like every day ordinary love becomes a palpable treasure with surprises and tangible bits that turn words into illumined art like colored glass when the light shines through. The Snapshot Celebration of Lesbian Love is a stretching of connective tissue through sisterhood, energizing and re-inventing as of yet untold stories of our love--like a lightning rod or a beacon, its expression luminous.

Renate on Susan

It is impossible to find words to describe what 33 years of being Susan Hawthorne's partner and living together has been like. Perhaps if I were an ancient poet, beautiful words would flow on the page ... beautiful words for a beautiful woman. But as a mere 21st century mortal I struggle. Where to begin? Which Susan to describe? For she has so many alter egos and each of them comes with her own special delight and quirkiness. Circus performer, both scaring and delighting me with tissu drops from far too high up. Publisher, with an admirable talent for new ventures, new angles and above all a dedicated tenacity even when the going gets rough. Political and intellectual warrior, always standing up for lesbians and feminists – and the wild – the marginalised of this world. Poet, reciting for me her gorgeous words sometimes daily especially in the year of the daily poem. Source of wisdom, from ancient languages to ancient women to metaphysics and black holes – is there anything this woman doesn't know? Animal lover, co-'mother' of our special dogs, River and Freya; sharing my deep grief and despondency when both of them left us. Tropical rainforest and plant lover except when vines are concerned: Tarzana-like she forces them down. Best friend – here words totally elude me – Susan's daily kindness, Susan's daily support, Susan's great meals, Susan's humour, Susan's contagious energy to keep going, often against the odds. Fun and adventure when we go bush and camp. I know I have her back and she has mine. It's been heartfelt love and commitment for 33 years during sunshine and rain (even cyclones). I know a love like this is rare and I treasure the rarity Susan Hawthorne is: an extraordinary talented Renaissance woman with a heart of gold who I am lucky enough to call my soul mate and lover.

Renate

Susan on Renate

You are the kindest and most generous person I've ever met. When we met at Sandra's party in 1986 we talked and talked. Soon I was suggesting you be invited to the Women's Ball. I wore my heart pants. How obvious can you be? But our lives were still on opposite sides of the world and so we waited. That first year, so hard with so little time together but when we were we laughed a lot. I decided I had to learn German although it was not necessary. I am still learning. But you can walk into a room and shift across multiple languages easily. I love that when we travel you are more interested in the welfare of dogs whose photos you take, occasionally in front of some tourist landmark, more often among the street rubbish on the footpath. This love of dogs and of anyone who is facing difficulty in her life is such an important part of you. Your serious sense of justice combined with your ability to be magnificently silly is fantastic. Such joy, so many books and our joint publishing work have made it an incredible journey. I feel so lucky to have shared almost half my life with you, whether we are living in one another's pockets or separated by thousands of miles. You are always right there.

I wrote the following poem for Renate on her 64th birthday.

Sixty-four
for R

I dream you as a song
on the day you turn sixty-four.
Will you still love me? you sing

in reminiscence of old songs
of days when you and I were both young.

I dream you as a poem
and when you smile
you seem not as old as sixty-four
but a young thing
full of mischief and irreverence.

I dream you as a play
of light and shade
and gathering moods
when you are sixty-four
and the dog wags her assent.

I dream you as a work of art
coloured bright
with pinks, orange and red
hardly the colours of one
who is sixty-four.

5 April 2009

'Sixty-four' was first published in the anthology *Press: 100 Love Letters* edited by Laurel Flores Fantauzzo and Francesca Rendle-Short. Quezon City: The University of the Philippines Press, 2017.

Photo by Lariane Fonseca

BOOK REVIEWS

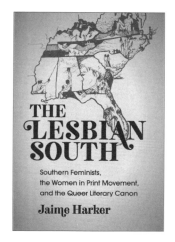

The Lesbian South, by **Jaime Harker**
The University of North Carolina
Press, Chapel Hill
Paperback, 201 pages, $25.90

Reviewed by Roberta Arnold

Sometimes at odds and sometimes united, an unlikely posse of southern lesbian feminist publishers, writers, activists, and landykes stride through the frame under Jaime Harker's lintel and are met by a scholar's scrutiny and the open arms of familial embrace. From letters, archives, and those still living in community, Harker's descant of southern lesbian feminism is a dulcet serenade combining methodical research and uncloaked truth in an essential contribution to history. Harker catalyzes schools of thought taking place in the second wave in four chapters. First, the outposts of two writing styles: the feminist avant-garde at one end and the accessible narrative on the other, conjoining into *The Women In Print Movement* and the *Battle of the Literary* to frame *Lesbian Feminist Culture*. Second, *The Radical South*, defined by *Politics and the Lesbian Feminist Imaginary*--although sometimes manifest within Southern contradictions, connects directly to the roots of southern civic rebellion, detailing how lesbian feminist activism in the south included intersectionality. Third, *Queer Southern Sexuality and the Lesbian Feminist South*, recognizes the transgressive within unique definitions of southern lesbian feminist writing in order to nose out imposed southern stereotype. Marking the powerful plantings of lesbian strongholds in the south, *Women's Space, Queer Space, Communes, Landykes, and Queer Contact Zones* reveals the fourth catalyst within lesbian feminist literature and venue, where the LGBTQ community staked their claim to inhabit fear-free zones in the south.

During the brio rising up from the women's movement in the 70s, southern lesbians were not afraid to claim their place at the table. Barbara Grier and June Arnold take the catbird seat, as two "important midwives," (p 18), who published consequential lesbian feminist writers of the time. Harker describes Grier's place in history as an embrace of the non-elitist world of "accessible narratives, especially for lesbian readers," (p 18). Arnold, perching on the opposite book end, welcomes a rebirthing of the "feminist avant-garde," (p 18).

Although Grier and Arnold presented "as antagonists, they were... co-conspirators as well," (p 18). By bookending these two publishers/writers, Harker frames the southern lesbian feminist tenet: *Politics and the Lesbian Feminist Avant-Garde*, (p 21). "For Arnold, the exclusion of women in general, and lesbians in particular, from the literary canon led her to theorize a specifically lesbian feminist version of the literary, marked by experimentation and by feminist politics," (p 18).

Grier also valued the lesbian literary, and included "the popular for the cultural work it performed, especially for lesbian readers," (p 18).

Bertha Harris joined forces with Arnold and Daughters, Inc. by 1973, shortly after the press began in the 1971, and together Harris and Arnold distinguished their mutual embrace of the lesbian aesthetic, defined in their writings as "esoteric fiction," and the "literary avant-garde," (p 42). Favoring an earlier avant-garde movement in lesbian writings, they drew inspiration from the generation before them, including Natalie Barney, Gertrude Stein, Radclyffe Hall, and Virginia Woolf (p 29). This appreciation went side by side with the political message of the time: *the personal is political*. The books published by Daughters, Inc. evidenced this philosophy, publishing *The Cook & the Carpenter*, by June Arnold in 1973 and *Confessions of Cherubino*, by Bertha Harris in 1978.

Grier, embracing literary and popular writing, published Shelia Ortiz Taylors's *Faultline,* and Katherine Forrest's "highly successful" *Curious Wine.* Judy Grahn, Rita Mae Brown, Kate Millet, and Sarah Schulman all published with Grier during this time.

Harker considers writing examples from several southern lesbian feminist writers to illustrate the four-point tenet. Writing characteristics creating the Southern Lesbian Feminist Culture included gender variant identities as in Arnold's, *The Cook & the Carpenter*, and a poetic lesbian feminist political consciousness including activism and intersectionality.

In Minnie Bruce Pratt's *Crime Against Nature*, first published in 1989 by Firebrand Press, and later reissued as a Sapphic classic by *Sinister Wisdom* and *A Midsummer's Nights Press* in 2013, Pratt gives poetic voice to the personal experience of losing her children because she is a lesbian. Spreading literary wings to form an iconic lesbian *cri de couer*, Pratt's poem expresses what the 70s lesbian feminists embraced: an activist stance against oppressions of class, sex, race, and being lesbian. Pratt would bring to the foreground class and race determinants in the south through her teachings as well as her poetry. Moreover, Pratt and her soon-to-be spouse, Leslie Fienberg, would radically redefine gender expression and class-consciousness through Marxist theory, anti-racist action, and their written work. Pratt publically thanked the WIP movement, lesbian culture, and the LGBTQ community when she won The Lamont Poetry Prize for *Crime Against Nature* in 1989: "I would not have begun to live as a lesbian nor have survived to write these poems without the women's liberation and the gay and lesbian liberation movements.... Women who've excavated and saved the facts of lesbian history, women who've written the poems, edited the magazines,

148 ♀ Sinister Wisdom 112- *Moon and Cormorant*

newspapers and journals, taken the photographs, taped the radio shows, run the bookstores, and begun the women's studies and gay studies programs, women who have created the places for lesbians to think and live and flourish," (97) (p 54).

This recognition marked an apex celebration of lesbian culture into the mainstream and led to Dorothy Allison's nomination as a 1992 finalist for The National Book Award for *Bastard Out of Carolina*.

Pratt collaborated with Cris South and Mab Segrest to work on a lesbian feminist periodical that began from a collective of lesbian feminists in Chapel Hill in 1974, as *The Feminist Newsletter*--and then became *Feminary*, a lesbian feminist literary magazine. A photo of the collective is included in the mid-section, just after page 98, along with the notable *Feminary* pictorial map of the south in a collage of intimate lesbian scenes, illustrated on Harker's paperback cover, first published in *Feminary* by Sue Sneddon. More photos from that era reprinted in this midsection are likely to make us old lesbian feminist hellcats warm with nostalgia.

When Harker describes women writers beginning at the genesis of the 70s print movement, the relationship is personal. Like a smooth stone, sculpted by sand and salty sea, thrown with a practiced hand, spinning out and up from a clear surface, skipping forward, circle upon circle extending, each one traced by their own notable waves. She recreates these voices as they were. As Bertha Harris is quoted saying: "The great service of literature is to tell us who we are.... Lesbians.... Unassimilable, awesome, dangerous, outrageous, different, *distinguished*.... Monstrous," (p 34).

First read at the MLA and later published in the *Sinister Wisdom* Issue on *Lesbian Writing and Publishing*--put together by Beth Hodges (Volume 1, Issue 2; 1978), Arnold's essay: *Feminist Presses and Feminist Politics* speaks to the notion of defining lesbian feminist writing characteristics. "We've experimented with unpatriarchal spelling and neuter pronouns. I think we've changed our sentence structure, and paragraphs no longer contain one subject... the inclusiveness of many complex things.... Experience weaving in on itself, *in*clusive, not ending in final victory/defeat, but ending with a sense that the community continues," (p 34).

Lesbian feminists held many personal and public debates where exchanged words would run roughshod over a person in defense of politic ideals, thereby defining themselves and their stance. In Harker's dissemination, all of these positions come into an alignment not realized at the time:

"Women's liberation was a combative, simultaneous, and complicated braid of multiple conversations, movements, and manifestos," (p 9).

The beginning days of the first Women in Print Movement conference--started by Arnold on index cards sent out to the multitude of feminist bookstores, presses, magazines, distributors, reviewers, editors, and writers--spotlights Harker's chronicle of lesbian feminist culture, born for the purpose of inclusion and strategizing about keeping the community alive. "Daughters, Inc.'s inclusive tendencies became apparent in June Arnold's most important activist legacy: the formal creation of what is now called the Women in Print Movement," (p 39).

Sinister Wisdom's beginnings in 1976, recounted from letters and "Nicholson's extensive hand-written notes from the many practical sessions at the first WIP (Women in Print) conference in 1976 (still preserved in the Sallie Bingham Center at Duke University) showed that the sessions provided mentorship," (p 41).

Chapter Two describes the history of southern radicalism which led into the activism and intersectionality of southern lesbian feminists. In part inspired by the civil rights movement, and in part by an independence that had come to categorize southerners as rebels, Harker dispels the idea that intersectionality in southern history is wish fulfillment. Harker widens the lens on southern lesbian feminist history and lists the examples of a south fighting for civil rights. "African American activism that focused on the sexual assault of black women by white men; (5) the beginnings of

150 ♀ Sinister Wisdom 112- *Moon and Cormorant*

the black power movement in Lowndes County, Alabama; (6) and early feminist organizing (7)," (p 60).

Rose Norman provides Harker plenary documentation of lesbian feminist activism in the south, as cited in the *Sinister Wisdom 93: Southern Lesbian-Feminist Herstory* 1966-1994, (p 62). These lesser-known accounts of southern history included anti-Klan activism and labor organizing. "From the creation of women's resource centers and women's studies programs... to the establishment of battered women's shelters and rape crisis centers to legal battles over reproductive rights, domestic violence, rape laws, custody of children, child care, and the Equal Rights Amendment, southern feminists were involved in the full range.... issues of economic inequality, mass incarceration, animal welfare, and what we now call "critical race studies," (pgs 62-63). Informing their community on racism, southern lesbian feminists sought to transform power relations between white women and women of color, while simultaneously delivering a boot kick to patriarchy. "We keep forgetting these eruptions of the radical South in our literature and our history, but they inform the southern lesbian feminist writers of *The Lesbian South*," (p 61).

Cris South's 1984 novel, *Clenched Fists, Burning Crosses* "considered the connection between anti-Klan activism and feminism. The epigraph to the novel comes from Pat Parker's essay "*Revolution: It's Not Neat, Pretty or Quick,* which places the Klan in a systemic feminist critique of a patriarchal society: The Klan and the Nazis are our enemies and must be stopped," (43) (p 76).

Harker's upending of southern lesbian feminist history brings individual and collective contributions together to actively work against racism in community.

"This understanding of the interconnections of sexism, racism, and homophobia was broadly embraced in a 1980s lesbian feminist culture that continued to include southern lesbian feminists. The feminist journal *Conditions*, started by four white lesbian feminists, focused its fifth issue on African American writers including southerners Ann Allen Shockley and Pat Parker. That issue, Julie Enszer maintains, had enormous influence, selling out print runs (10,000 copies) and inspiring the publication of germinal essay collections listed above. It also led to the transformation of the *Conditions* collective into a multicultural collective that featured Cheryl Clarke, Jewelle Gomez, and Dorothy Allison." (67, Enszer, "*Fighting to Create*," (pgs 89-90).

The poems of Pat Parker illustrate a deep blaze of perception in the southern radical lesbian feminist. In the poem: "The *What Liberation Front?*"

Parker brings humor, pathos and layered insight to the movement:

> Today I had a talk with my dog
> he called me a racist—chauvinist person
> told me he didn't like the way
> I keep trying to change him....
> and property—he wanted to know why
> people expected dogs to protect their capitalist interest
> he never watches television or plays
> records. & how come I put tags on him.
> my dog – he laughed. He is his own dog.
> and what's this bullshit about his sex
> life. If he wants to fuck in the streets it's
> his business. (28, Parker, *Pit Stop*) (p 62)

Harker provides several poems by Parker as rare examples of lesbian feminist humor during the 70s, and the defining lesbian feminist position on relationship with animals: rejecting animal as property, (p 68) and including their needs as paramount. The southern lesbian feminist narrative uncovered in Parker's poems brings many issues to the foreground: "racism within queer communities; homophobia within black communities; white supremacy and its devastating consequence," (p. 71). In Harker's analysis of Parker's poems, their collective impact is a landmark.

"Parker's seemingly simple poetry is actually extraordinarily nuanced and layered and performs often dangerous critiques of normative American society," (p 68).

Pat Parker, Rita Mae Brown, Blanche McCrary Boyd, June Arnold, Dorothy Allison and Minnie Bruce Pratt are just a handful of writers defining lesbian feminist activism in the Radical South. "As lesbians, these southern writers placed themselves beyond the boundaries of "acceptable" southern ladyhood," (p 63).

In Minnie Bruce Pratt's *Rebellion: Essays 1980 – 1991*, the lesbian feminist critique of oppression, Harker further illumines the radicalization of southern lesbian feminism. "That "deep connection" of oppression—of racial and religious intolerance, and the ways that accusations of "perversion" serve to keep others in their place—helped Pratt to critique the injustices of her southern upbringing. This intersectional critique marks the archive of southern lesbian feminism... Deconstructing the status quo led to complex radical coalitions," (p 64).

In Chapter 3: Queer Sexuality and the Lesbian Feminist South, Harker elucidates Dorothy Allison's understanding and embrace of marginal people in the south as allied with Bertha Harris. Allison is more forthcoming than most in her embrace of transgressive sexuality: the controversial, held by Allison, is emboldened by its political position. "Allison ties the grotesque to the marginal in the South—African Americans, lesbians, and the poor; if that grotesque interpolates all these groups as deviants, then Allison embraces that label, in solidarity with all the South's cultural others," (p 102).

Harker exposes transgressive sexuality as a line of resistance for the Southern lesbian feminist. From the grotesque, to the monster, written images become an avenue of cultural expression and freedom. Harker unmasks this complexity in writings by the southern lesbian feminist and asserts that these transgressions "challenge patriarchy and suggest more empowering sexual roles for women; to shock and invert the negativity surrounding the "decadent southerner"; and to expose the ways that "deviant sexuality" is actually a tool of the status quo," (p 103).

In Chapter 4: Women's Space, Queer Space: Communes, Landykes, and Queer Contact Zones in The Lesbian Feminist South, Harker questions the assumption in LGBTQ communities of the "metronormativity" of queer life, (p 141). "Early women's liberation was long engaged with challenging the patriarchal hierarchies of space, both public and private," (p 143). As evidenced by gay bars, music festivals, communes, and land that women inhabited in the 70s, Harker integrates rural lesbian feminist community into her analysis of *Women's Space, Queer Space*. Citing examples of imagined lesbian society in the following novels: Sally Gearhart's 1978 novel *The Wanderground*, June Arnold's *The Cook and the Carpenter*, Elana Dykewomon's *Riverfinger Women*, the 1975 science fiction novel by Joanna Russ, *The Female Man*, and *Lover* by Bertha Harris: "All imagine women's worlds as less violent, more equitable, more diverse, and more in tune with the wider natural world than the patriarchy," (p 147).

I was struck by Harker's summation of how print culture, online community, and activism, now included progressive religious organizations. Perhaps this is a survival tool. Grier and her partner, McBride, sold the original TL mailing list, along with the Naiad Press backlist, to Bella Books, continuing romance and mystery genres, (p 190).

"*Sinister Wisdom* is still publishing; now led by editor and poet, Julie Enszer, it is one of the few remaining institutions creating lesbian feminist community, and true to its roots, it has published three special issues on lesbian feminism in the south, all of which have been instrumental in the writing of this book," (p 190).

In the spirit of a newly rising lesbian feminist south, Harker opened her own gay bookstore smack dab on Main Street in Mississippi; brazenly naming it: *The Violet Valley Bookstore*. Southern lesbian literature includes social activism to this day,

154 ♀ Sinister Wisdom 112- *Moon and Cormorant*

Harker informs: "queer activism still continues to be widespread, especially in the South. Marriage Equality has provoked a vicious backlash in southern states. And organizations like the Campaign for Southern Equality are resisting this backlash.... This activism is coalitional with Black Lives Matter and progressive religious organizations joining with queer activists to resist institutional racism, sexism, and homophobia," (pgs 194-5).

If you know where to look, Southern Lesbian Feminists have left their watermark. *The Lesbian South* by Jaime Harker tells us precisely where to look, providing analysis and history not found anywhere else. In Harker's book, the community of Southern lesbian feminist writers have left their legacy. Harker has passed this along with genuine respect and inclusivity.

"The creation of a South grounded in different ideologies and notions of power, one in which "radical," "queer," and "southern" are not mutually exclusive, is the most lasting legacy of Southern lesbian feminist writers in their exploration of radical politics, transgressive sexuality, and queer space," (p 9).

The life force of lesbian rebel women ride into the present with familial embrace and well-documented, careful construction. An astonishing gift of inspiration for teachers, scholars, and students--and those of us who were there.

"In The Lesbian South, I reconstruct a history of a group of writers, who when remembered at all, tend to be approached in isolation. These sassy, talented, resourceful, and often hilarious southern lesbian feminists deserve to be remembered as the remarkable tribe they were.... Part memoir, part literary history and criticism, but it is, finally, a love letter to the South – my South... full of sexual deviants and political radicals, scalawags and carpetbaggers, potheads and drunkards, embracing racial mixing, excess, an unadulterated kindness," (p 16).

In Harker's ride through the lesbian feminist south, rejuvenation occurs. A collective of individuals threaded through the reins in Harker's hands—sometimes in the style of Belles-Lettres, an immediacy of the personal, and sometimes in the traditional fact-finding mission of the scholar. All hats off to Harker: the southern lesbian feminist posse rides again.

They:
A Biblical Tale of Secret Genders
by **Janet Mason**
Adelaide Books, New York - Lisbon
Paperback – March 11, 2018;
286 pages, $22.30

Reviewed by Roberta Arnold

I magine a scribe that lived during biblical times. Imagine she was an enlightened woman: pagan, inclusive--with an ability to recount allegories of myth and religion from a different perspective. All this in fluid prose rolling smoothly through ancient and modern thought, including lesbian and intersex lives with mystical matrilineal vision. Imagine that this amanuensis, friend to animals, and storytelling teacher, who sees how much of the world is barred from her, recreates and reinvents herself to find a way to teach and live throughout time. The price of disobedience, her life: adventure, travel, teaching and knowledge, only for men. From this imagined scribe comes the captivating story of two sisters, Tamar, the elder by minutes, and her twin sister Tabitha. The scribe begins as the woman named Tamar. Tamar lives in a tent in the desert of Egypt where she holds teachings of the ancients for the women of the neighboring village. The teachings are not the usual stories of the Bible in the historical period of Judah and Joseph: they include many gods,

156 ♀ Sinister Wisdom 112- *Moon and Cormorant*

not just the one, a pagan view of nature and animals, and lives that are born intersex and gender-fluid.

The two sisters are oppositional, the contrast in characters illumining differences of perception. In the biblical story read to them by their Great Grandmother, the story of Creation remembered and retold demonstrates an example of these differences.

"I've been thinking about this for a while. She pulled a thin blanket up to her skin. Great Grandmother told us that God created Adam and Eve in his image. That meant that God must be male and female, not just male like we thought," (p. 48).

"I'm not sure Great Grandmother had the story right," said Tamar, shaking her head. Auntie Namaah told me the same story from the serpent's point of view. In her story, God was female and remembered the old ways. God was just pretending to be male, because the men wanted Him to be male just like them," (pgs. 48-49).

A longer excerpt of the story of Creation from *They* can be found on page 118 of *Sinister Wisdom 100: Anniversary*.

Mason seamlessly writes story, intermixing different religions with her own allegory. From the Hebrew Bible: Joseph seeing into the future. From Mesopotamian times in Sumerian religion: the goddess Innana/Istar; a different female model of power—one who is not vengeful and interested in adornment, but is thoughtful, kind, and still powerful--and the handmaiden who rescues her as a 2-spirit guide with power born from quiet action and seeing the bigger picture. Even to a novice religious eye like mine, parallels to Hebrew and other religious teachings are redolent as they unfold throughout the book. Written in colloquial story-telling style and delightfully told--like a mother reading fairytales to her children at bedtime. From her *Wordpress* home page, we learn that Mason's inspiration for this book is from the Gnostic Gospels:

The Gnostic Gospels were discovered in the Egyptian town of Nag Hammadi in 1945. Originally written in Coptic, these texts date back to ancient times and give us an alternative glimpse into the Gospels that are written in the New Testament. They are so important that they are banned in some conventional religions. And in my book, that's a good reason to read them....The Gnostic Gospels have provided me with inspiration for my writing, particularly in my novel THEY, a biblical tale of secret genders.... I am inspired by the Gnostic Gospels in part because they let in the light. In particular, they let in the light of the feminine.

Tabitha, the younger sister, gives birth to intersex twins in Tamar's tent. Tabitha is seen contentiously by Tamar, as a creature of impulse and untaught instinct—but she often catches herself— female competition and harping on fault is a trick played on them, injected by a patriarch who wants to keep them powerless as a group and to keep his control over them. Tamar is the teacher, the stolid practical mind who knows from the start that knowledge, independence, and self-sufficiency will bring her inner strength and keep her safe. She teaches from scrolls of knowledge passed on to her by a traveler from another land. From these scrolls, she teaches about the many goddesses and gods people have prayed to, including animal totems.

Judah, residing over the kingdom of Judah, is the patriarch, wed to Tamar although he happily lives in his own dwelling of riches with his maidservant Milcah. Judah becomes the father of the intersex twins born to Tabitha—not by his own seed however. He is father by proxy. Tabitha falls in lust upon viewing the naked upper torso of a village shepherd she sees in passing—having sex with him in the pasture. When Tabitha becomes pregnant, the two sisters devise a plan to keep the pregnant Tabitha safe from being burned at the stake, along with a way to keep the twins well-cared for by the well-to-do Judah. Tamar is to trick Judah into thinking that she is a harlot on the road, beckoning Judah to come to her. Judah doesn't need much beckoning and quickly jumps at the game plan. From a hidden vantage point for witnessing the event, Tamar watches with detached curiosity as her sister is "pumped"

158 ♀ Sinister Wisdom 112- *Moon and Cormorant*

by Judah. This is another indication that Tamar is not your average heterosexual female. Judah provides for his children when they turn up in Tamar's tent, thinking they are sons of his own. It is a convoluted complicated scheme but one that works because the men rarely look at women's faces and the women's faces in this case are veiled.

Tamar loves being alone and we soon discover along with her that her sexual inclinations are lesbian. She becomes a vegetarian because of her close relationship with her two goats, and her camel, Aziz--who sleeps inside the tent in order to protect him from the ravages of desert windstorms and predators. Tamar also notes that he is getting old: she can tell by the expansion of his knobby knees. Behind Tamar's tent the two goats live in a garden among cultivated olive trees and herbs. The table Tamar prepares for the seduction of one of the women in her circle (who attends teachings from the scroll) is a spread of olives, goat cheese, oiled bread, pomegranate, and figs. They drink wine from silver wedding goblets and feed each other until they have had enough of the food but not enough of each other.

"Let me feed you," said Judith. She picked up an olive, held it between her fingers. Then she broke off a piece of the oiled bread. She reached out and fed it to Tamar. Tamar felt Judith's cool fingers on her lips. When she was done, Tamar fed Judith. They saved the fresh figs for last," (pgs 112-113).

Tabitha's intersex children are raised by their two Aunts. The stories they are told are of myth, legend, religion, and sometimes magic. There is the legend of Ishtar who visits the underworld with her spirit guide to see her sister, the queen of the underworld. The spirit guide, Asushunamir, saves the goddess Ishtar from death in the underworld because anyone who enters there does not come back. A bas relief of Ishtar is shown to the twins when they are little. Ishtar looms large in their eyes like a female superhero and the Aunts steer the twins to the hidden power of the story.

"Asushunamir was male and female – just like you. Without Asushunamir there would be no story," (p 64).

When the children are looking at the bas relief of the goddess Ishtar they want to know where her wings are as well as her penis; this starts a conundrum of questions from them about whether Ishtar's penis got broken off or whether they would grow breasts when they grew up.

"The important thing to remember is that you should never be ashamed of your body. Just remember, though, that not everyone feels the same way. They don't understand and they might hurt you," (p 64).

This only opens up more questions for the twins: *why would anyone hurt them?* When their mother explains that people are afraid, the twins want to know: *why are they afraid?* (p 64). This leads to a theme that Mason repeats more than once in the book: how religion can control people.

"The priests teach them to be afraid," said Tamar. "They teach that it is better to have a son than a daughter, even though it's not true. The priests control who the property goes to when someone dies. This way they amass more wealth for themselves. If a man dies, the property goes to the priests and not to his wife. The woman is the man's property. If the husband dies, she is expected to marry or become a family member's servant. None of this is right of course. Women are just as smart as men. This is just how the priests keep their power," (p. 65).

In this modern, provocative, deeply layered book, Mason presents allegory as powerful knowledge: how far or how little we can see and use this knowledge—depending on perspective—tells us how far we have come or how far we have to go--perspectives are the choices written between the lines. Illuminating a different kind of spiritual guide, born from matrilineal teachings and ideas passed down and remixed into an inclusionary spirit of today, Mason uses exquisite story-telling skills to envision a place where a more just and equal world can co-exist with all its differences.

As the premise of the LGBTQI movement as coalitional goes, our alliances with different genders, colors, and religious belief--from the mystical to the agnostic to those deeply rooted in traditional culture, and the matrilineal female culture, there is much to discover; Mason teaches us with a grace and vision as exquisite as it is otherworldly fun.

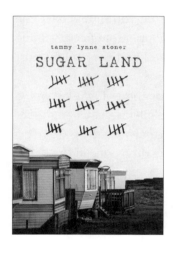

Sugar Land
by **Tammy Lynne Stoner**
Red Hen Press, 2018
344 pages, $16.95

Reviewed by Sarah Heying

Most of us have that one relative (or seven) who is slow on the sensitivity uptake and resistant towards self-reflection; the one who casually throws around racist, sexist, or homophobic language and laughs off any opposition as yet more proof that the world (a euphemism for people of color, queer and trans folk, women, people with disabilities, etc.) has no sense of humor. This relative might infuriate us with their willful ignorance, but they also remind us of where we could be if we had not followed our more virtuous and open-minded path. "They'll never change," we might say. "They're stuck in the dark ages."

But as Tammy Lynne Stoner shows us in her debut novel *Sugar Land*, sometimes people do change, even very late in life. The narrator, Dara, is born in 1903, and takes years and years of doing everything wrong before she figures out how to do a few things right. The novel carries readers from Dara's time working in a men's prison in Texas in the 1920s through her eventual life as a retiree in the sixties and seventies, a period of radical change in views towards gender and sexuality. Dara's earnest struggle to change with the times while holding onto meaningful traditions transforms her from *that one relative* to a lesbian ancestor who deeply understands the nuances of succumbing to harmful societal norms for survival's sake.

Sugar Land is organized around the development of Dara's identity from just plain Dara to Miss Dara to Nana Dara to Mrs. Dara, and her personal twist on each honorific variously conforms to and redefines the expectations of her community. It is a development told in retrospect, as Dara only becomes the first-person narrator of her own life story later in life, after she's reckoned with herself enough to reflect on her past with honesty. Yet aside from the first chapter, the novel proceeds chronologically, and so Stoner layers time and memory primarily through perspective rather than plot-- Dara's older selves commune with her younger selves as a supreme feat of self-actualization. From Dara's first love for an open and adventurous young woman named Rhodie, to the violent intrusion of her small southern hometown's politics, to Dara's escape from herself in the walls of a prison, to her mid- and late-life journey towards self-acceptance and genuine love of others, this coming of age story lasts a lifetime.

This structure is reminiscent of *Stone Butch Blues*, and like Feinberg's picaresque, the crass but loveable narrator spends decades growing into and outgrowing ever-changing identity categories, eventually learning to be honest about what's gained and who gets left out when joining a "We." Though Dara's honesty is blunt, the way she communicates through idiomatic language of her own creation pays homage to Fannie Flagg's layered colloquialisms that both play into and push the boundaries of southern stereotypes. Dara's nerves jump "more than a grasshopper on a griddle," and she names her prefab home the

Bland Ole Opry. And just as Flagg's boundary-pushing sneaks in behind a mischievously congenial "bless your heart," *Sugar Land* offers sweetly packaged, light commentary on race, class, and trans identities.

This mixture of heavy and light-hearted content is at its best when it allows both Dara and the reader to look head-on at highly controversial issues, such as Dara's unlikely friendship with her roommate at the Bland Ole Opry, a man she dubs The Fiddler for his obsession with tinkering with any object within arm's reach. Yet the moniker has a more serious association, as the Fiddler is a reformed pedophile who frequently associates his own urges with Dara's attraction to women, much to her chagrin. They are a duo who understands each other's shame, but who can never seem to help each other move forward. "Somehow I made him say to me perhaps the things I thought of myself," Dara confesses. "I hurt him to hurt me."

Ultimately, *Sugar Land* is deep-fried, gin-soaked, love-filled story about reckoning with some of the worst of mistakes while also realizing the astounding human capacity for growth. Though Dara clings to some of her wilder beliefs, such as her certainty of an impending alien abduction, she slowly learns to peel away layers of internalized shame and secrecy that lead her towards self-loathing and manipulation of others. Dara's capacity for reflection might remind readers of the ways in which we all have been, or continue to be, *that one person* in some form or another, and how a simple shift in perspective can cause a windfall of growth. "No life is easy, and no life is hard;" Dara muses, "it's just what adjectives you choose to describe it."

A Certain Loneliness: A Memoir
by **Sandra Gail Lambert**
University of Nebraska Press,
210 pages, $19.95

Reviewed by Roberta Arnold

A Certain Loneliness by Sandra Gail Lambert is a treasure: at times poetic and rhapsodic, at times witty and wry, the sum total is a brilliant tribute to the trials and triumphs of a body living with polio, to everyday lesbian life, and to a love affair with nature. Describing in a writer's voice what it means, how it feels, and how other's respond to a body with limited physical abilities--as a body on crutches, a body in a wheelchair, and sometimes, beautifully expressed, as a body getting in and out of a kayak, Lambert has given us a treatise on disability that spotlights the physical abilities it takes to compensate for the waning muscles of polio, the gumption it takes to fight social discrimination-- and the self-reflections of this body being one with nature. Each story carved out in natural essay form is more than a memoir. Like Thoreau's, *On Walden Pond*, except with a lesbian sensibility--and in my opinion better written, a singular voice flows through the complicated maze of a life like a running brook. Lambert gives us a set of keys to unlock complicated human dilemma, making this book more of a *roman à clef* than memoir. Like Plath's *Bell Jar*, personal experience is combined with a writer's narrative. The voice is numinous, satirical, visceral, and abundant.

The daughter of a disciplinarian military father and a life-coach mother, the first page describes an early memory combining beauty in nature with its startling ominous counterpart. The six-year-old Lambert crawls down a hill at the edge of the forest and takes in the beauty of the flowers growing there, lily of the valley.

"Deep in the woods was a place the sun reached to the ground, and at the edges of light, in its shadow, the flowers spread over the forest floor. I'd sit among them and smooth the skirt of my dress around me. The bare skin between my panties and the top thigh band of my braces pressed into the wet slickness of the ground. The white pearls of flowers about to open would perch on my fingertips, and they seemed to have no weight. Cars, construction, my mother's voice, and the confusion of where to sit on the school bus or why no one sat with me and the relief of reaching the classroom and the kindness of the teacher also lost any substance. The honey perfume of the disturbed plants rose around me.

It turns out that lily of the valley and all its parts—stems, roots, flowers, leaves—are poisonous. It slows the heart." (P. 1).

Lambert's childhood is spent in a corset made of plastic. When the army transfers her father to the states, the surgeries are scheduled there; steel rods will be inserted into her body. In Sweden during the fifties, the benefit of socialized medicine allows the family to make an appointment with a doctor before they leave for America. The doctor recommends fierce physical exercise. Lambert stretches the power of her muscles under the guidance of an ex-Olympian swim teacher. The swim practice is daunting, but the young Lambert is determined and encouraged and meets the physical challenges head on with proud success. She has passed a milestone.

After the surgeries in the States, a six-month stay in the hospital is required. Lambert's mother is only allowed to visit her in the hospital for an hour a day. We bear witness to the pain of this time as so unbearable it becomes existential angst: referring to herself as "the child," and "well-nourished white child," displayed on the chart at the foot of the bed. This out-of-body existence teaches Lambert to learn with her eyes and her voice--telling stories to her stuffed rabbit, and keeping alive her love affair with nature.

The essays are not always chronological. Subject and lessons learned string together with a symmetry of recalled experience. An episode in the beginning is set in a laundromat: a woman pounces on the girl in the wheelchair doing her laundry--the cringe-worthy patronizing words spilling from the woman's pious righteousness fall onto the bound audience. We are right there with the girl as she pretends to reel in her clothes, waiting for the woman to leave, her head deep into the dryer.

The writing is exact and fluid. I found myself sailing along so fast I had to force myself to stop so I could re-read paragraphs in order to savor every word. There are episodes of lesbian potlucks that are sure to ring familiar; a demonstration in Disney World in the 90s called *Poster Children* that is priceless.

"We're in single file led by an American flag with stars in the shape of a wheelchair," (pgs. 59-60). And then, in Orlando, inside the front lobby of a Disney World hotel for white tourists who wear primary colors in shorts and tops, an ADAPT action. "ADAPT is a group of disability rights activists who believe people are better off living in their own homes," (p. 60). The demonstration ends when everyone is arrested.

"The police department's strategy had been to arrest every able-bodied person they could. They figured these people could act as attendants in jail. It was ADAPT's policy that they should refuse," (p. 60). What follows is step-by-step instruction on how to lift, position, and then reposition later by a woman whose sister watches with her arms crossed leaning against the wall— told to a pair of policemen who follow along until the tasks are completed.

In another essay, Lambert explores the survival instinct of withdrawal into oneself--in lesbian relationships and in single life, she describes the physiological pathway of the lesbian body reeling inward, happening at the cellular level.

166 ♀ Sinister Wisdom 112- *Moon and Cormorant*

At her comedic best, Lambert mulls over whether or not it is time to get a dog.

"Was I to become another aging single woman who had dogs to hug and call sweet names instead of developing a real relationship? There I was on another Saturday night watching videos on Pet Finders. 'I'm Trixie. I love playing hard and need to find somewhere to let myself go.' And, "I'm Dahlia. I'm a shy girl but a cuddler once you get to know me.' That's when I saw her. I called a friend to intervene.

'Are you looking at those pet porn sites again?' he asked, (pgs. 133-134)."

Lambert's sense of whimsy takes me to a delicious place of play like the lesbian relationship of a world within a world. The unself-conscious caprice leads to laughter that can't be held in—bursting forth with pent up blissful release.

Lambert's physical embrace of nature is like a relationship with a lover without having her disability defined. The complicated planning of getting into a kayak and back out and up on the wheelchair by herself is a strategical set of maneuvers freely executed when no one is watching. Like the kayak rides, the future cost of the body's pain is worth the unleashing of this desire. Nature, embraced like a lover, becomes one with Lambert, another description so perfect we feel the earth as she sinks into it.

"I lie on my back, knees bent. A thin skin of water ripples down it. My legs flop to the side, my hip follows, and now my breasts are against the earth. My body mixes the wilted grasses with the soil. I roll again, and my shoulders sink into the smoothness of dissolving plantain leaves. I spread my arms and rotting grasses wrap around them.... My knees are the last part of me pressed into the watery earth of Paynes Prairie," (pgs. 41-42).

Lambert's respect for nature threads throughout the book. On kayak trips, she peels all the hard-boiled eggshells for her friends, knowing how easy it is to sprinkle eggshell bits into the river: her commitment to leaving the earth as she found it. Through the sterling voice of this brilliant wordsmith, we bear witness to the struggle and grace of a lesbian body undiminished: the relationship with other lesbians and nature so beautiful, daring, and necessary for survival, the heart reverberates with applause.

CONTRIBUTORS

Jane Bartier is a visual artist working particularly in response to place – Jane asks, what are our understandings of place, and how does place activate enquiry? From her practice of walking and looming she makes, from materials at hand, another landscape, markers of new maps. Her work has been exhibited at the Deakin University Waterfront Gallery, the Perth Institute of Contemporary Art, and RMIT March. She is currently a PhD candidate at Deakin University.

Winifred D. (Wynn) Cherry began teaching in Patrick County, VA and continued her career at Broughton High School in Raleigh, her Alma Mater. At Broughton she initiated the International Baccalaureate Program and began Proyecto Quetzal, an international study and service program in Guatemala. She retired in 2009 and served on the board of Friends of FUNDAL, supporting deaf and blind children in Guatemala. She earned a BS in English and a BA in Appalachian Regional Studies from Appalachian State University, a MA in English from NCSU, and a PhD from UNC-Chapel Hill with her dissertation *Outlaws with Charm: The Evolution of the Southern Lesbian Voice*. Wynn lived in Durham, NC with her partner, Elizabeth, and two children, Tatiana and Torres. She died in December 2015.

Michelle Cliff (1946—2016) grew up in Jamaica and New York City; she studied at Wagner College in New York and at the Warburg Institute in London. She worked as an editor at Time Life and at W.W. Norton, where she edited *The Winner Names the Age*, a collection of writing by Lillian Smith. Beginning in in 1981, she and Adrienne Rich co-edited *Sinister Wisdom* until their move to California in 1984. For many years Cliff taught writing at Trinity College in Massachusetts, and published nearly a dozen books including fiction, poetry and prose.

Marisa Crane is a lesbian writer whose work has appeared in *Hobart, Jellyfish Review, Pithead Chapel, Drunk Monkeys, Pidgeonholes, Switchback, X-R-A-Y Magazine,* and elsewhere. She currently lives in San Diego with her wife. You can find her on Twitter @marisabcrane.

Chanice Cruz is originally from Brooklyn, New York and has lived much of her life in Richmond Virginia where she became involved with Slam Richmond. She was a founding member in its first youth slam team Slam Dominion. She has performed in several states including, Louisiana, Oklahoma, New Mexico, Arizona, and California. She is currently enrolled in the creative writing program in Nassau Community College and will be graduating with her associates degree in 2019.

Marilyn Hacker is the author of thirteen books of poems, including *A Stranger's Mirror* (Norton, 2015) *Names* (Norton, 2010), an essay collection, *Unauthorized Voices* (Michigan, 2010), and sixteen collections of translations of French and Francophone poets including Emmanuel Moses, Marie Etienne, Vénus Khoury-Ghata, and Habib Tengour . *DiaspoRenga,* a collaborative book written with the Palestinian-American poet Deema Shehabi, was published by Holland Park Press in 2014. She received the 2009 American PEN award for poetry in translation, and the international Argana Prize for Poetry from the Beit as-Sh'ir/ House of Poetry in Morocco in 2011. She lives in Paris. These new poems will be published in *Blazons,* to appear with the Carcanet Press, U.K., this spring.

Mie Astrup Jensen is a MA Sociology student at the University of Aberdeen, Scotland. She specialises in intersectional feminism; specifically, gender, sexuality, race, ethnicity, and religion. Her dream is to become an academic activist specialising in women's- and LGBTQ+ rights, thus combining her love for academia and

170 ♀ Sinister Wisdom 112- *Moon and Cormorant*

real-life activism to advocate for social justice. Through reading and writing as a teen, Jensen began exploring and understanding her sexuality. Jensen has never taken any creative writing classes, but was encouraged by people to write her feelings, so she fully allows her feelings to lead the pen. Her works have appeared on *DIVA*, *OpenDemocracy*, *The Write Launch*, and *The Gaudie*.

Yeva Johnson, a Black American Jewish Lesbian feminist mother and musician, is an emerging poet who works as a physician by day. Her father, an electrical engineer and poet, encouraged Johnson to write poetry in childhood, but it was difficult to indulge this passion as an adult. In December of 2014, supported by her first mentor, Johnson recommenced writing poems and has written a poem a day since. Johnson is a member of the QTPOC4SHO artists' collective for queer and transgender artists of color in the Bay Area that includes visual artists, performance artists, writers and comedians. Through poems, she explores the life cycle, social hierarchies and interlocking caste-systems, the possibilities for interconnection, nature, love, and all that is fleeting. Johnson lives in Northern California.

Emel Karakozak was born in Turkey in 1974. Her adventure in photography started in high school. She has participated in many group exhibitions, received awards in various national and international competitions and also was jury member in many photography competitions. Living in Adana, she is the first woman in Turkey who has EFIAP/g title and who opened her first personal exhibition 'Lotus' in 2010 in Adana Sabancı Fine Art Gallery. She opened her second personal exhibition in Istanbul Artgalerim. She also worked in 2012 Art Bosphorus Contemporary Art Fair, 2011 Contemporary Istanbul Contemporary Art Fair, 2011 Art Bosphorus Contemporary Art Fair. Her works were took place in Hacettepe Art Museum and BAKSI Art Museum and also in and Romantic Bad Rehburg Museum and in Steyerberger Rathaus Germany,

Vittebsk/Belarus Center for Contemporary Art, Cultural Center of the Zdwina and Museum of Kreises. She worked at Artgalerim Nişantası Art Gallery as a photograhpy artist for 3 years and she contunies her carieer as photography artist at Artgalerim Bebek Art Gallery and Lust Auf Kunst Art Gallery. She works as a federation delegate and federation in TFSF (Turkish Federation of Photographic Art).

Kaye Lin Kuphal is a transracially adopted Chinese American lesbian living with her fiancée in Pearl City, Hawaii. She graduated from Colgate University with a BA having majored in biochemistry and minored in creative writing. Her writing seeks to respect the complexity of truth, womanhood, queerness, ethnicity and culture, poetry, scientific precision, the moment when observation determines actuality, continuance, art and music, and the life force. She considers all sewer cats to be her own.

Jenna Lyles is a multi-genre writer based in The Deep South, where she lives with her better half and works toward an MFA in Creative Writing. Her poetry appears or is set to appear in *Breakwater Review, Juked, Calamus Journal,* and other such publications. You can—and she hopes you will—find her at jennalyles.com.

Rosita Angulo Libre de Marulanda is a Colombia (S.A.) born lesbian writer and poet. She was transplanted to the U.S. when she was thirteen years of age, at the cusp of womanhood. She's a 40-year activist in various liberation movements as she has experienced discrimination on many points of intersection including gender, race, age, sexual preference, physical, emotional, and financial challenges. Rosita is launching her own business, Rosita's Kitchen, under which she has done workshops at GRIOT and Women Writers in Bloom on how to start a barbecue fire without using lighter fluid and how to take the next step towards healthier eating. She's coming to terms with being transgender by shedding the feminine gender assigned to her based on her female genitals. Please call her Gender Free! She lives in Brooklyn, New York.

Rita Mookerjee's poetry is featured or forthcoming in Aaduna, New Delta Review, GlitterMOB, Berfrois, and Cosmonauts Avenue. Her critical work has been featured in the *Routledge Companion of Literature and Food*, the *Bloomsbury Handbook to Literary and Cultural Theory*, and the *Bloomsbury Handbook of Twenty-First Century Feminist Theory*. She is a PhD candidate at Florida State University specializing in contemporary Caribbean literature.

Minnie Bruce Pratt's first book, *The Sound of One Fork*, was self-published with the help of queer women in 1981; a new edition organized by Julie Enszer is at http://www.lesbianpoetryarchive. org/sites/default/files/SOOFEEditionFINAL.pdf. Pratt's award-winning *Crime Against Nature* is available in a new Sinister Wisdom-sponsored edition at A Midsummer Night›s Press.

Ashley-Luisa Santangelo is a first generation Colombian-American, born and raised in Pennsylvania. She works in a library by day and is a writer and an artist by night. Her poetry and short stories have been featured in *The George Street Carnival* and the *Storymaker's Association*. In 2015, she was awarded the Academy of American Poets Student Prize for her poem, *Frida*. She graduated with an honors B.A. in Latin American Art History from Hunter College in 2018.

Alaina Symanovich holds an MFA in Creative Writing from Florida State University and an MA in English from Penn State University. Her work has appeared in *Quarter After Eight*, *Sonora Review*, *Superstition Review*, and more. Find her at alainasymanovich.com.

Yasmin Tambiah grew up in Sri Lanka, and lived there intermittently during the years of war between the Sri Lankan Government and the Liberation Tigers of Tamil Eelam. She has also spent long periods of her adult life in the USA and Australia, with stints in England, India, Spain and Trinidad. Trained as a European medievalist, she now investigates issues at the crossing points of law, gender and sexuality in postcolonial states, and works in research management. Her creative writing has appeared in *Conditions* (New York), *Nethra* (Colombo), *ZineWest* (Western Sydney) and *Sinister Wisdom*; anthologies edited by Joan Nestle and Yasmine Gooneratne; and elsewhere. She has won awards for writing from the Astraea Lesbian Foundation and ZineWest. She currently lives in Sydney, Australia.

Lila Tziona began writing at a very young age. She has attended two writer's workshops, one during the summer of 2013 at Wake Forest University in North Carolina, and another during the summer of 2014 at Georgia Tech. She is currently an undergrad at University of Toronto, and plans to major in psychology. Lila takes inspiration from authors such as Jane Austen, whose writing influenced her own style after first reading *Emma* at age ten, as well as the stream-of-consciousness style of writers like Virginia Woolf.

Red Washburn, PhD, is Associate Professor of English and Director of Women's and Gender Studies at Kingsborough Community College (CUNY). They also are Adjunct Associate Professor of Women and Gender Studies at Hunter College (CUNY). Red's articles appear in *Journal for the Study of Radicalism*, *Women's Studies: An Interdisciplinary Journal*, and *Journal of Lesbian Studies*. Their poetry collection *Crestview Tree Woman* was published by Finishing Line Press. They co-edited the *Sinister Wisdom*: *A Multicultural Lesbian Literary and Art Journal* issues *Celebrating the Michigan Womyn's Music Festival* and *Dump Trump: Legacies of*

174 ♀ Sinister Wisdom 112- *Moon and Cormorant*

Resistance. Red is a coordinator at the <u>Lesbian Herstory Archives</u> and of the <u>Rainbow Book Fair</u>.

Julie Weiss received her BA in English Literature and Creative Writing from San Jose State University. She is a lesbian poet, originally from Foster City, California, who moved to Spain on a whim in 2001 and never looked back. She works as a telephone English teacher from her home in Ciudad Valdeluz, a developing Spanish ghost town, where she lives with her wife, 4-year-old daughter, and 1-year-old son. Her poetry has been published or is forthcoming in *Lavender Review, The American Journal of Poetry, Glass: A Journal of Poetry—Poets Resist Series, Stonecoast Review*, and *Peculiar*, among others. Julie translated this poem and read it to her wife during their wedding ceremony, in her finest American-accented Spanish. You can find her on Twitter @colourofpoetry or at https://julieweiss2001.wordpress.com/.

Christina M. Wells is a Professor of English at Northern Virginia Community College. She holds an MA from University of Arkansas, Fayetteville and a PhD from University of Maryland, College Park. She has also studied writing at Sewanee Writers' Conference and in Christina Baldwin's writing circles. Her work is published or forthcoming in *Rough Copy, Story Circle Journal, Northern Virginia Review*, the blog of New Ventures West, *Crab Fat Magazine, bioStories*, and *Big Muddy*. She is currently circulating her first novel and writing her second. While she is originally from Arkansas, she has lived in the D.C. metro area for twenty years. She and her wife live in Northern Virginia with their three cats and one dog.

Spring 2019　175

Sinister Wisdom
A Multicultural Lesbian Literary & Art Journal

SUBSCRIBE TODAY!

Subscribe using the enclosed subscription card or online at
www.SinisterWisdom.org/subscribe using PayPal

Or send check or money order to
Sinister Wisdom - 2333 McIntosh Road, Dover, FL 33527-5980

Sinister Wisdom accepts gifts of all sizes to support the journal.

Sinister Wisdom is free on request to women in prisons
and psychiatric institutions.

Back issues available!

Sinister Wisdom **Back Issues Available**

111 Golden Mermaids ($14)
110 Legacies of Resistance: Dump Trump ($14)
108 For The Hard Ones.
    Para las duras ($18.95)
107 Black Lesbians—
    We Are the Revolution! ($14)
104 Lesbianima Rising: Lesbian-Feminist
    Arts in the South, 1974–96 ($12)
103 Celebrating the Michigan Womyn's
    Music Festival ($12)
102 The Complete Works of Pat Parker ($22.95)
    Special Limited edition hardcover($35)
98 Landykes of the South ($12)
96 What Can I Ask ($18.95)
93 Southern Lesbian-Feminist
    Herstory 1968–94 ($12)
91 Living as a Lesbian ($17.95)
88 Crime Against Nature ($17.95)
87 Tribute to Adrienne Rich
84 Time/Space
83 Identity and Desire
82 In Amerika They Call Us
    Dykes: Lesbian Lives in the 70s
81 Lesbian Poetry – When? And Now!
80 Willing Up and Keeling Over
77 Environmental Issues Lesbian
    Concerns
76 Open Issue
75 Lesbian Theories/Lesbian Controversies
73 The Art Issue
71 Open Issue
70 30th Anniversary Celebration
65 Lesbian Mothers & Grandmothers
63 Lesbians and Nature
58 Open Issue
57 Healing
54 Lesbians & Religion
53 Old Dykes/Lesbians – Guest
    Edited by Lesbians Over 60
52 Allies Issue
51 New Lesbian Writing
50 Not the Ethics Issue
49 The Lesbian Body

48 Lesbian Resistance Including
   work by Dykes in Prison
47 Lesbians of Color: Tellin' It
   Like It 'Tis
46 Dyke Lives
45 Lesbians & Class (the first issue of a
   lesbian journal edited entirely by
   poverty and working class dykes)
43/44 15th Anniversary double-size
   (368 pgs) retrospective
39 Disability
36 Surviving Psychiatric Assault/
   Creating emotional well being
34 Sci-Fi, Fantasy & Lesbian Visions
33 Wisdom
32 Open Issue

- Sister Love: The Letters
  of Audre Lorde and Pat Parker ($14.95)
- Lesbian Badge ($2.50)
- Lesbian Bomb Poster ($20)

Back issues are $6.00
unless noted plus $3.00
Shipping & Handling
for 1st issue; $1.00 for each
additional issue.
Order online at
www.sinisterwisdom.org

Or mail check or money
order to:
Sinister Wisdom
2333 McIntosh Road
Dover, FL 33527-5980